Implementing Hoshin Kanri

Implementing Hoshin Kanri

How to Manage Strategy Through Policy Deployment and Continuous Improvement

Anders Melander, David Andersson,
Fredrik Elgh, Fredrik Fjellstedt, Malin Löfving

Translated by Rikard Ehnsiö

Routledge
Taylor & Francis Group
A PRODUCTIVITY PRESS BOOK

First published 2022
by Routledge
605 Third Avenue, New York, NY 10158

and by Routledge
2 Park Square, Milton Park, Abingdon, Oxon, OX14 4RN

Routledge is an imprint of the Taylor & Francis Group, an informa business

ISBN: 978-1-032-04826-0 (hbk)
ISBN: 978-1-032-04825-3 (pbk)
ISBN: 978-1-003-19481-1 (ebk)

DOI: 10.4324/9781003194811

Typeset in Garamond
by Apex CoVantage, LLC

Contents

Authors

Anders Melander is an associate professor in business administration at Jönköping International Business School. Anders researches and teaches strategic change, business development and strategy work. He has extensive experience in practicing business development and action-based research, especially in collaboration with small and medium-sized companies.

David Andersson has worked with strategic development for two decades in the role of leader and consultant, both professionally and as a volunteer. His focus is on creating an ability to change. Over the past five years, David has worked together with researchers at Jönköping University on developing effective methods for strategic development processes.

Fredrik Elgh is a professor of product development at the School of Engineering, Jönköping University. Fredrik has held various management positions in the area of education and research for more than a decade. He has a great deal of experience in research and development work in close collaboration with the industry, and he has worked actively with Hoshin Kanri for six years.

Fredrik Fjellstedt has a master's degree in business administration and economics with a focus on strategy and leadership. Fredrik has over ten years of experience with regard to lean thinking, leadership development and Hoshin Kanri at Toyota. He is the first person outside of Japan to become a master trainer in Toyota's eight-stage problem-solving method, and he has coached over 1,500 leaders. Today, Fredrik works as a senior enabler with a focus on Hoshin Kanri.

Malin Löfving has a PhD in technology management and economics. She works as project manager at Träcentrum Nässjö Kompetensutveckling AB and as an adjunct lecturer at the School of Engineering, Jönköping University. Malin conducts research on manufacturing strategies and production development in small and medium-sized enterprises.

Introduction

Welcome to our book on how to implement Hoshin Kanri! Here we summarize the results of a project that has been in progress for more than eight years and involved 28 companies and other organizations. The five of us working on the project are researchers, practitioners and consultants. We are all driven by a conviction that strategy work represents an important process where there is also great potential for improvements. We hope that this book will guide you in realizing this potential in your organization.

The book is based on Hoshin Kanri, a Japanese method for working with strategy. This method is not particularly well known and has so far mostly been used in multinational corporations with origins in Japan and the United States. In our project, we have tested whether Hoshin Kanri works in other contexts as well. Our answer to this question is "Yes, but it requires some adaptations." This need for adaptations when introducing the method is the reason we decided to write this book. So, our goal is not only that after reading the book you will have learned more about Hoshin Kanri, but also that you will be inspired to introduce the method in your own strategy work.

Those of us who have worked on this project are convinced that the principles forming the basis of Hoshin Kanri address current demands, and we hope that after reading this book, you will agree with us and start your own experimentation.

In the first chapter, we ask the first and perhaps most important "why-question": why should you work with strategy (according to Hoshin Kanri, or at all)? We then briefly describe what Hoshin Kanri is and how it differs from traditional ways of working with strategy. In Chapter 2, we discuss the visionary target condition of an organization working with Hoshin Kanri. In other words, we describe the principles guiding an organization fully devoted to working with Hoshin Kanri. In Chapter 3, we advise you on how you, our reader, can analyze the current condition with regard to strategy work. The analysis in Chapter 3 and the visionary target condition in Chapter 2 serve as the point of departure for choosing a challenge-based strategy for introducing Hoshin Kanri. The point of departure in Chapter 4 is that Hoshin Kanri is introduced gradually by addressing various challenges.

In Chapters 5 and 6, we abandon the challenge-based step-by-step introduction of Hoshin Kanri to instead assume that the organization introduces the entire Hoshin Kanri annual cycle in one move. We make this jump partly because it enables us to present how Hoshin Kanri works as a whole and partly because it describes a more "radical" introduction of Hoshin Kanri, which may be suitable for some organizations (however, we recommend the step-by-step introduction). Then, Chapter 7 offers a somewhat more detailed description of a number of analytical tools.

Last but not least, we have included a case—the Lindbäcks Group. This case is found in an appendix at the end of the book, but we recommend that you begin by reading it. This case gives you a sense of what strategy work according to Hoshin Kanri consists of and thus also a sense of which type of journey we discuss in the book. Throughout the book, we also illustrate our reasoning by examples, which in most cases originate from organizations participating in our research project[1] or our courses. Many thanks to Vinnova[2] for having funded our research and dissemination activities.

By having read this far, you have already been introduced to two important principles in Hoshin Kanri. The first is *process orientation*:

1. Always start by asking the question "Why?" In this case, "Why work with strategy?" (Chapter 1)
2. What does the (visionary) target condition look like when working with Hoshin Kanri? (Chapter 2)
3. What does your current condition look like? (Chapter 3)
4. How are you to move from the current condition to the target condition? (Chapter 4)
5. An in-depth discussion on how Hoshin Kanri works as well as relevant analytical tools (Chapters 5–7)

The second basic principle is that in Hoshin Kanri, you work *based on facts* and do not focus on the solution from the outset. In practice, this means that if you are interested in Hoshin Kanri, you *can't* skip Chapters 1–3 and immediately start implementing the solutions in Chapters 4 or 5. The message in this book is that a thorough fact-based analysis of the current condition saves time in the long run. So, take the time to read and continuously reflect upon your organization before you start experimenting.

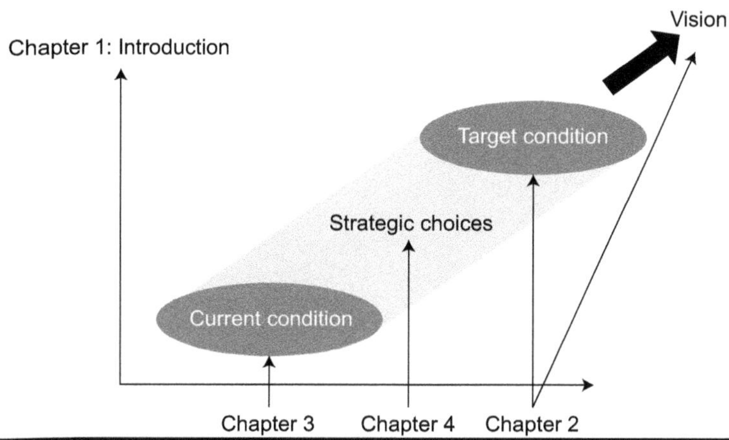

Figure I.1 The Process Orientation in Hoshin Kanri

This book is not very long, but we hope that its message will stay with you for a long time. Once again, welcome to our book on how to implement Hoshin Kanri!

Anders Melander
David Andersson
Fredrik Elgh
Fredrik Fjellstedt
Malin Löfving[3]

Notes

1. The Vinnova-funded research project focused on Hoshin Kanri in small and medium-sized manufacturing companies. We concluded that the ideas in Hoshin Kanri work in both large and small contexts, but that the main question concerns how this approach is introduced. This result led to our step-by-step model in Chapter 4, in which Hoshin Kanri is gradually introduced by addressing specific strategic challenges.
2. Vinnova is a government agency under the Swedish Ministry of Enterprise and Innovation.
3. Many thanks to Mikael Thulin and Stefan Österström for valuable input in previous phases of this project.

Chapter 1

Why Work with Strategy According to Hoshin Kanri?

> Having a strategy suggests an ability to look up from the short term and the trivial, to view the long term and the essential, to address causes rather than symptoms, to see woods rather than trees.
>
> **(Freedman 2013 p. ix)**

Lawrence Freedman wrote about the history of strategy in a book of more than 600 pages, but the preceding quote neatly sums up what strategy is all about. At the heart of strategy is a desire to combine the work of addressing everyday challenges with an ability to raise one's perspective and identify the overall way forward. The ability to balance short-term problem solving (operational level) with a long-term idea regarding the future (strategic level) has always been important, and there are many arguments for working systematically to maintain a productive balance between these two tasks.

Unfortunately, this balance is lacking in many organizations. Daily problem solving has taken over and long-term strategic work has been neglected. There are many reasons why this imbalance needs to be addressed and why the relationship between day-to-day issues and long-term strategic questions needs to be more productive. Here, we briefly address two reasons that it is becoming increasingly important to work systematically with strategy: value to customers[1] and engaged employees. We argue that these reasons are absolutely crucial for all organizations.

DOI: 10.4324/9781003194811-1

The fact that all organizations need to deliver something of *value to their customers* is obvious. However, the ongoing digitalization of society means that satisfying customers has become more challenging. Digitalization is making it increasingly easier for people to identify and evaluate alternatives. When buying products, customers are now able to sit in their office or on their couch and compare prices from a wide range of providers worldwide, while those utilizing health services, for instance, can choose between going to a primary care clinic or using a digital healthcare service when they become sick. If you are to survive as a provider of products or services in a situation where your customers have more and more choices, you obviously need to develop more valuable offerings to your customer than your competitors do. So, how are you going to achieve this? Wouldn't it be great to have a well-considered and structured strategy process utilizing the creativity of the entire organization to develop innovative solutions?

"The creativity of the entire organization" can be translated into *employee engagement*, the second reason that you should work with strategy. In this area, you're lucky! Current employees want to be more involved, they want to be able to influence their daily work, they want to understand how their organization can contribute to a better world and how they themselves may contribute in their work. This is a very positive development. Many brains think better than a single brain does. But things will get even better since there is great potential. Gallup's recurring "State of the Global Workplace" reported in 2017 that the average portion of engaged employees in the 155 countries surveyed was 15 percent (see Box 1.2 at the end of the chapter). So, the potential is enormous. And, if we agree that activities in the organization must be organized so they can benefit from the willingness of employees to contribute to overall growth, then the "only" question is: How do we achieve this?

We are not the first to reflect upon whether the traditional way of working with strategy is in line with our current society. In his 2018 book *Opening Strategy*, Professor Richard Whittington discusses how strategy work has developed since the 1960s. He argues that the traditional way of working with strategy, known as strategic planning, faced competition in the 1980s from a more learning-oriented approach, known as strategic management, and that a third alternative, known as open strategy, emerged in the 2000s. Whittington uses two terms to discuss the level of openness in strategy work: *inclusion* and *transparency*. These concern the number of people in the organization being included in the strategy work and management's level of transparency in strategic issues. We return to Whittington's reasoning later.

A conclusion from this overview is that strategy work can be designed in many different ways, and to open up your strategy work, you don't necessarily have to work according to Hoshin Kanri. But why should you reinvent the wheel? Hoshin Kanri has been tested in large organizations for almost 60 years. A company often referred to when discussing Hoshin Kanri is one of the largest car manufacturers in the world: Toyota. Toyota is a role model in lean philosophy and is almost always referred to in discussions on developing the area of production. A less-well-known fact is that Toyota uses the same basic principles when working with strategy:

> Hoshin (Kanri) is a key component of the Toyota Management Framework. It connects leadership's vision, values and philosophies (the Toyota Way) to the daily activities on the floor (developing people in problem solving to reach business goals).
>
> **(Liker & Hoseus 2008 p. 429)**

Hoshin Kanri is sometimes translated as a management compass in the Anglo-American literature since it concerns the ability of the entire organization to contribute to its overall objective and direction (Figure 1.1).

These words can also be interpreted as Hoshin addressing the planning phase, and Kanri addressing the execution and evaluation phase.

The basic principles of Hoshin Kanri and lean are the same: a conviction that correctly executing the method leads to the desired result. Management is here responsible for developing and continuously improving the method together with the employees. This focus on the method is frequently lacking in the strategy work of many current organizations.

However, there are important differences between Hoshin Kanri and lean. In the latter, the focus is on *continuous improvement efforts*, and

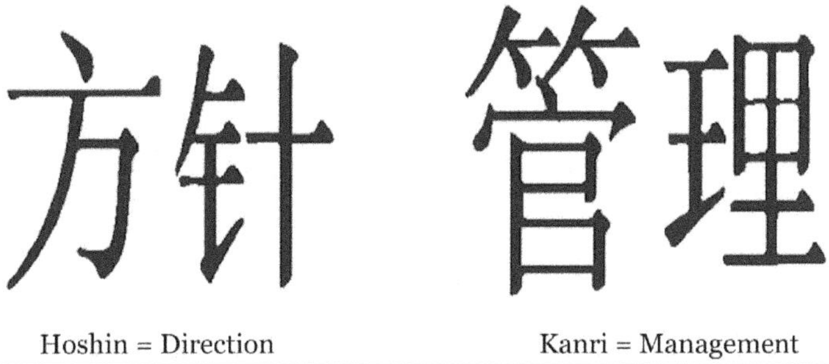

Figure 1.1 Meaning of the Term Hoshin Kanri

development efforts are driven by deviations from an established standard (Figure 1.2). The basis of this approach is that you should always work according to a defined standard and identify opportunities for continuous development within the framework of the current standard. In Hoshin Kanri, on the other hand, it is about taking a bigger leap and overcoming the obstacles preventing the organization from moving from the current condition to the target condition. In other words, this concerns a *vision for the future.* This vision is formulated by someone (owner, management), after which it is broken down into short-term target conditions. The obstacles that make up the gap between the vision and the current condition are often referred to as the organization's strategic challenges, or "hoshins." The ways of overcoming these obstacles are developed in discussions within the organization in a process of breaking these down into objectives. The literature on Hoshin Kanri often refers to terms such as catchball and deployment.[2]

But even if there are differences between Hoshin Kanri and lean, surely an organization with established, continuous improvement efforts according to lean would be in a better position to introduce Hoshin Kanri? No, according to our experience, it is not obvious that effective and continuous improvement efforts simplify the process of working with Hoshin Kanri. This is because continuous improvement efforts often are applied only in relation to production, whereas management has not adopted these values and methods. In Hoshin Kanri, management plays a crucial role.

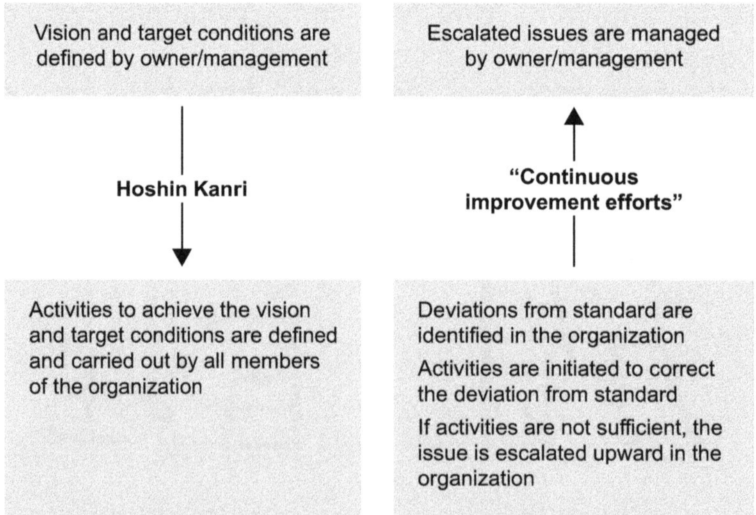

Figure 1.2 Hoshin Kanri and Continuous Improvements

Hoshin Kanri is thus a system for developing the entire organization in terms of strategy. As stated by Whittington (2018), the dominant system for developing organizations remains *strategic planning*. Initially, the difference between Hoshin Kanri and traditional strategic planning is not very significant. Both are based on performing a thorough analysis of the current condition, followed by defining a target condition/vision.

The difference between Hoshin Kanri and strategic planning becomes clearer in the next phase. The basis of Hoshin Kanri is that based on the vision, management identifies a few overall challenges that are crucial for realizing the vision. These are then broken down in the organization in the annual planning cycle. Hoshin Kanri thus assumes that management formulates *what* is to be achieved, but also that it, together with the employees in the organization, determines *how* it is to be carried out. In classic strategic planning, management decides both *what* to do and *how* to carry it out (i.e., the actual action plan). Only then is the remainder of the organization involved in terms of implementing the decisions made by management. To be honest, how stimulating is it to simply do what you are told without having any impact and without really understanding why it should be done?

BOX 1.1 VISIONARY STRATEGY WORK

One of our courses included representatives from the management team of Saab Training & Simulation, a business unit within the Saab Group. Within the course they launched a project to develop their strategy work according to Hoshin Kanri. They formulated the following vision:

Vision for the Strategy Work

We are a strategy-driven company, where every employee understands the company's strategy and uses it actively in their daily decisions.

It is worth noting that they were quite ambitious when formulating their vision. Every employee was included in the vision. The goal is that everyone understands the strategy so that they use it actively in their daily work. In other words, they need to understand in order to translate the strategic phrases into their work. This represents a significant step away from the traditional approach, where employees only need to understand how they are to implement what has been decided by management.

The rest of this book is about how you can introduce Hoshin Kanri in your organization. How do you identify a visionary target condition for the strategy work in your organization? How do you create a systematic approach for breaking down a vision together with your employees at different levels? How do you come to an agreement with your employees in terms of what to do over the next year? How do you follow up the different elements of Hoshin? How do you create a way of learning in order to develop the system?

The basic notion in the answers to all these questions is that when you introduce Hoshin Kanri, you must *apply the principles of Hoshin Kanri*. This may seem obvious. Still, it is often a forgotten principle in change work. Practicing what you preach is not always easy, but it is absolutely necessary for the credibility of the change efforts. In other words, it concerns gradually creating an understanding and engagement with regard to the approach. You can't order your organization to work with strategy according to Hoshin Kanri. Such an authoritarian approach is contrary to the principles.

Earlier, we wrote about Gallup's recurring "State of the Global Workplace" as we discussed employee engagement in organizations. We now return to this point. When we read this Gallup report, we started thinking—is the level of engagement really this low? However, even though the reported levels of engagement intuitively come across as low, this report inspired us to analyze this further. We know that participation leads to engagement. How do you create more participation? Gallup offers a few suggestions. Active inclusion in the strategy work (e.g., through the Hoshin Kanri methodology) is a further suggestion presented in this book.

BOX 1.2 ENGAGED IN YOUR WORK?

In Gallup's 2017 study "State of the Global Workplace," only an average of 15 percent of the respondents in 155 countries reported that they were engaged in their work. In addition, 18 percent of the respondents were actively dissatisfied with their work. The participants in the study had indicated that they had a full-time job, which was about one-third of the workforce.

There were substantial geographical differences. The respondents in Latin America and the United States and Canada were the most engaged

(27–31 percent). In Western Europe, this figure was 10 percent, and the least engaged employees lived in China, Japan and Hong Kong at 5–6 percent. Norway was the highest in Western Europe at 17 percent.

In terms of individual companies, Gallup identified engaging companies in all regions. Companies exhibiting a high level of engagement were also very successful with regard to other metrics, such as productivity, sales and profit. It is difficult to determine whether engagement leads to these results or whether it is the other way around.

The report operationalized engagement as follows:

Engaged: Employees are highly involved in and enthusiastic about their work and workplace. They are psychological "owners," drive performance and innovation, and move the organization forward.

Not engaged: Employees are psychologically unattached to their work and company. Because their engagement needs are not being fully met, they're putting time—but not energy or passion—into their work.

Actively disengaged: Employees aren't just unhappy at work—they are resentful that their needs aren't being met and are acting out their unhappiness. Every day, these workers potentially undermine what their engaged coworkers accomplish (p. 22–23).

So, how do you achieve a higher level of engagement? Gallup points out a fairly common strategy. One that does *not* encourage engagement:

> Creating a culture of engagement requires more than completing an annual employee survey and then leaving managers on their own, hoping they will learn something from the survey results that will change the way they manage.
>
> **(p. 44)**

Instead, they emphasize that engagement requires

> an organization to take a close look at how critical engagement elements align with their performance development and human capital strategies.
>
> **(p. 44)**

Finally, Gallup identifies a number of factors characterizing organizations with engaged employees:

> They know that engagement starts at the top. Highly engaged organizations have highly committed leaders. . . . They communicate openly and consistently, and they actively work on identifying and removing systemic barriers that prevent managers and employees from doing great work. They place the utmost importance on using the right metrics and hiring and developing great managers. Leaders of great workplaces also model the kind of psychological ownership that characterizes high engagement, visibly working to improve their own performance day by day.
>
> They know local managers are in key positions to support employees' engagement and productivity levels. Exemplary companies know that the experiences that inspire and encourage employees are local—they take place at the workgroup level. They hold managers accountable for outcomes. Great companies hold local managers accountable, not just for their team's engagement level, but also for how it relates to the team's overall performance.
>
> They ensure that basic engagement requirements are met before expecting an inspiring mission to matter. Only when employees know what is expected of them, have what they need to do their job right, are a good fit for their role and feel their manager has their back will they feel invested enough to connect with proclamations of mission or values—no matter how inspiring these might sound in the head office.
>
> They have a straightforward and decisive approach to performance management. Companies with the highest engagement levels use recognition as a powerful incentive currency for developing employees' capabilities.

They do not pursue engagement for its own sake. Highly engaged organizations stay focused on the outcomes associated with higher engagement levels, avoiding the survey trap described earlier (p. 47–48).

BOX 1.3 WANT TO LEARN MORE?

In his book, Richard Whittington describes in detail how strategy work has developed in large companies since the 1960s. If you work as a strategist, this is an excellent overview of how this field has evolved.

- Whittington, R. (2018), *Opening Strategy: Professional Strategists and Practice Change, 1960 to Today*. Oxford: Oxford University Press.

If you want to learn more about strategy from a historical perspective, Lawrence Freedman's book is very informative.

- Freedman, L. (2013), *Strategy: A History*. Oxford: Oxford University Press.

If you want to learn more about strategy and strategic issues related to warfare and politics, John Baylis et al. present a book delving into many topical issues.

- Baylis, J., Wirtz, J. J. & Gray, C. S. (2019), *Strategy in the Contemporary World*. Oxford: Oxford University Press.

Two books describing Toyota and its culture might be of interest. There are a few pages on Hoshin Kanri in these books, but the focus is on organizational values.

- Hino, S. (2006), *Inside the Mind of Toyota*. New York: Productivity Press.
- Liker, J. K. & Hoseus, M. (2008), *Toyota Culture: The Heart and Soul of the Toyota Way*. New York: McGraw-Hill.

Gallup's recurring study "State of the Global Workplace" is interesting reading. You can download the latest edition (2017) at: www.gallup.com/workplace/238079/state-global-workplace-2017.aspx.

Notes

1. Hoshin Kanri can be applied in all kinds of organizations. In this book, we use the term *customer* in order to simplify things. In a public organization, one may use terms such as "citizens," "users" or the like.
2. There are many terms one could use. For instance, Hoshin Kanri is also frequently referred to as policy deployment, where policy refers to strategy and deployment refers to dissemination. We return to the term catchball in Chapters 5 and 6.

Chapter 2

How Do You Recognize a Hoshin Kanri Organization?

In this chapter, we describe what a visionary target condition for Hoshin Kanri efforts may look like in an organization that has implemented this approach. Keep in mind that what is described here is actually a *visionary target condition*. This means that as far as we know, no organization has reached this condition, even though many seek to do so. We base Chapter 3 on the visionary target condition and create a checklist that you can use for analyzing the current condition of your organization. Once the current condition has been identified, you have also identified the need for change, as this is the gap you will work on bridging. A strategy for closing this gap is described in the following chapters.

First, however, a few words on the concept of visionary target condition. Facebook, one of the most famous companies in the world, has the following vision: "Bring the world closer together." There are obviously many opinions regarding the quality of this vision, but it is quite clear that without Mark Zuckerberg's long description (several pages) of what it means in practice, it might just as well be the vision of an airline or even a mobile network operator. Why, then, do management teams formulate visions at all if they turn out to be so vague? The obvious answer is that it concerns creating a vision of the future—something we should strive for together. However, one difficulty in formulating a vision is that it often must live up to several different and, to some extent, conflicting demands. It should be short and powerful, while at the same time offering guidance. Nor should it be too precise but allow for strategic alternatives. Hence, formulating a good

DOI: 10.4324/9781003194811-2

vision is harder than one might think. This may be one reason why many organizations spend a great deal of time formulating a vision, and then relatively quickly hide the result in some file cabinet.

By using a "visionary target condition," we want to emphasize the importance of the *guidance aspect* of the vision. By target condition, we refer to a description of how the organization operates when the vision has been achieved. For example, part of Coca-Cola's vision is that employees should look upon their company as "a great place to work where people are inspired to be the best they can be." But unless Coca-Cola specifies how to achieve this target condition, employees would easily end up looking at the employee element of the vision as nothing but an empty phrase.

Over time, we have come across many organizations that don't offer much guidance on how to achieve the vision, if they have even formulated a vision or objective to begin with. Nor does a vision specifying a certain turnover and profit in a given year offer much guidance, meaning that it is more or less meaningless. So, our recommendation is to either use a short and distinct vision, supplemented by a guiding document more clearly describing the target condition such as in the earlier Facebook example, or a more detailed vision that also addresses the target condition.

In the figure describing the structure of the book in the introduction, we used the dimension of time as we divided the visionary target condition into two parts. We indicated that the vision specifies the long-term direction and supplemented this with a target condition describing the state of things in a slightly shorter timeframe (e.g., five years), but later, we often use the term visionary target condition in a more general sense when we refer to long-term objectives. We return to an in-depth discussion on this topic in Section 7.2.

Regardless of which terms you choose to use in your organization when it comes to formulating the long-term objective, we would like to emphasize that we look upon formulating a target condition that offers clear guidance to the employees as the most important job of the owner/management. What all too frequently ends up being quite general and empty phrases must be filled with carefully considered content!

2.1 The Visionary Target Condition for Hoshin Kanri

The easiest way of analyzing whether an organization works according to the Hoshin Kanri methodology is to start with a checklist and check off whether all the recommended analytical tools are utilized. Does the organization have an overall vision? If they use one, check. Do they use tools 1, 2, 3 . . .? If they do, check. Daily management? If they do, check—and so on. This represents a fairly easy way of evaluating this question. It is clear and measurable. The problem is that there are different possible ways of working with all these analytical tools. For example, it is easy to formulate a vision and upload it to a website, but this obviously doesn't mean that all employees are familiar with the vision or that it has any effect on day-to-day operations.

A somewhat more difficult way of analyzing whether an organization is working according to Hoshin Kanri is to focus on how basic principles are applied in operations. If you do this, you will have a different type of checklist. Once the visionary target condition of Hoshin Kanri has been achieved, the organization should be characterized by the following seven principles:

- Long-term thinking
- Change curiosity
- Focus
- Process orientation
- Visualization
- Managing by learning
- Facts that drive and decide[1]

Our experience is that organizations need to reach a certain level of maturity based on these principles in order to be successful. In our research project, we found organizations that were mature based on the previous principles but which had achieved this state entirely on their own. We also found other organizations that had applied many of the tools that could be said to belong to the Hoshin Kanri toolbox but that felt that their strategy work had not been altogether successful.

The conclusion is that one should be careful to distinguish between the tools applied and the objective pursued. The previous principles may serve as a starting point for formulating your objectives, while the rest (the tools) are the means for achieving these ends. Next, we present a more detailed description of these principles to then link them to the overall approach—the scientific systematic approach.

2.1.1 Principle 1: Long-Term Thinking

For all organizations, it is essential to have a driving force or purpose that explains its existence. The primary aim for all organizations is to create value for the stakeholders, may they be owners, customers, employees or the common good in the society in which the organization operates. We usually describe this as the organization's idea or business idea. Furthermore, organizations tend to have an ambition: to grow, to be profitable, to be the best at what they do and so on. This objective may be referred to as the organization's vision. However, the terms in themselves do not matter here. What matters is the content. In larger companies and public organizations, the organization's idea and vision are often written down, while in smaller organizations, it is not uncommon that these thoughts only exist in the head of the owner or CEO.

As we suggested in the introduction to this chapter, the point of an organization's idea and vision is that they should offer guidance for the future. They will guide the strategy work. In many organizations, however, this long-term form of guidance is vague, and what determines how the organization develops is more up to chance. If, for instance, we listen to entrepreneurs who developed their companies from scratch, we find they often started with a specific problem that resulted in them developing solutions they could then scale up (see Box 2.1 for an example). This approach works in smaller and highly individual-based organizations. Once the organization has grown, however, this approach gradually becomes more difficult, and there is a need for clearer guidance.

> *We believe that a desire to systematically develop the organization toward a clearly formulated and communicated vision intending to create long-term value for the organization and its stakeholders is a fundamental prerequisite for being successful when adopting Hoshin Kanri.*

In this book, we stress this principle by referring to a clearly formulated and communicated vision as *visionary target conditions*. This is to emphasize the difference from the vague and rather nondirectional content communicated in most corporate visions.

2.1.2 Principle 2: Change Curiosity

In most organizations, a key to success is the ability to optimize existing work. You streamline, meaning that you seek to develop the organization by optimizing the way you utilize resources. Perhaps you can get your salespeople to visit one additional customer per day. Perhaps the cleaner can

BOX 2.1 PROBLEM-ORIENTED STRATEGY WORK

A while back, we went on a study visit to a Swedish fruit grower, where the CEO told us about the journey made by his family business. They had started selling their fruit on the town square but realized that there was no future in doing this. In addition, it was difficult to motivate the family to go into town every weekend and sell fruit. They then tried to launch a café and sell their fruit on the farm, which turned out to be very successful. They also collaborated with some stores to which they delivered fruit in boxes. Perhaps it was possible to expand this part of their company? After some thought, they chose to expand, and they now sell via weekly fruit deliveries in a large district. One day, however, when their blueberry client decided to buy blueberries from Poland instead, the company lacked someone buying a large portion of its products. That is when the idea to launch their own production of fruit drinks was born. With the changing climate affecting their fruit production, they have also started experimenting with growing grapes.

This is a story of challenges having materialized and being resolved, a story that many small business owners are able to tell. The company has now grown considerably with many different orientations, which, in turn, has resulted in more challenges (or opportunities) than ever. At the same time, it feels as if they have less and less time. The family must make more and greater choices. Which are the most important challenges/opportunities they need to prioritize? There is obviously a need for a guiding vision pointing out a target condition when making all these prioritizations!

clean an additional room if you improve the cleaning process. This type of behavior is necessary and often absolutely crucial for the organization to survive. It is no coincidence that lean management has become so popular. Lean represents an effective process for streamlining current operations. Focus on continuous improvements!

However, this may become a problem if your focus on *doing things correctly* results in you not thinking about *doing the correct things*. This leads to improvements within tight boundaries. In order to succeed when using Hoshin Kanri, it is necessary to not only optimize your current way of working but also to have a desire, be open to challenge and change your whole way of working. In a Hoshin Kanri organization, all employees dare challenge their current way of working. To achieve this, the organization's management must maintain an open mind so that untried ideas can be tested. The most important aspect here is not that all experiments lead to immediate success, but that everyone is encouraged to reflect upon and question the current way of working and thus become innovative. This is the basis for organizational learning.

> *We believe that organizations where employees are allowed and encouraged to challenge the current way of working are the ones that, in the long term, will do the right things. These are the truly innovative organizations.*

BOX 2.2 3M'S INNOVATIVE CULTURE

3M is often seen as one of the most innovative companies in the world. They are famous for their goal that 30 percent of sales should originate from products introduced in the market less than five years ago. William L. McKnight is considered the person behind 3M's innovative culture. The following quote describes his management philosophy introduced in the company in 1948:

> As our business grows, it becomes increasingly necessary to delegate responsibility and to encourage men and women to exercise their initiative. This requires considerable tolerance. Those men and women, to whom we delegate authority and responsibility, if they are good people, are going to want to do their jobs in their own way. Mistakes will be made. But if a person is essentially right, the mistakes he or she makes are not as serious in the long run as the mistakes management will make if it undertakes to tell those in authority exactly how they must do their jobs. Management that is destructively critical when mistakes are made kills initiative. And it's essential that we have many people with initiative if we are to continue to grow.[2]

Food for thought today, too, isn't it?

2.1.3 Principle 3: Focus

If you look for synonyms for "focus," you encounter words such as center, core and focal point. You also encounter expressions such as "emphasize" or "concentrate on." One quote attributed to Steve Jobs tells us more:

> People think focus means saying yes to the thing you've got to focus on. But that's not what it means at all. It means saying no to the hundred other good ideas that there are. You have to pick carefully. I'm actually as proud of the things we haven't done as of the things I have done. Innovation is saying no to 1,000 things.

So, focusing is about saying no. It is about choosing not to embark on a plethora of opportunities and concentrating on one or a few. All successful organizations (and people) have been good at focusing. They have chosen something to focus on and entirely concentrated on this. There are also those who choose to focus on being generalists, which may work well if there is a need for this. Think of an athlete specializing in pentathlon or heptathlon. In all other cases, a stronger focus is preferable.

Focusing is difficult. You can get a feeling of missing out on something when you make a choice, subsequently choosing not to do anything at all, even if you know that this is an even worse alternative. In addition, there is frequently some kind of notion of fairness found within organizations: we should all have something to focus on. This easily results in each function focusing on its own small challenge while no one focuses on the overall challenge facing the organization.

Steve Jobs also tells us another important thing in his quote when saying, "you have to pick carefully." When studying successful individuals or organizations, we discover that their focus has remarkably often been due to chance. Be that as it may, focusing occurs at different levels. One concerns the overall direction. Carolina Klüft,[3] former Olympic and world champion in heptathlon, started competing in track and field. Her focus on heptathlon was a coincidence. If her coach, who had a background in decathlon, had not lived in the Swedish town of Växjö, perhaps she would have focused on another discipline in track and field. However, chance at that level doesn't mean that it was a coincidence *how* Carolina practiced heptathlon. What led to her practice being focused was the result of carefully analyzing her strengths and weaknesses. Just like any organization, Klüft did not possess infinite resources. She had to prioritize—sorry, focus.

To continue the Klüft analogy, focusing often results in new opportunities. If you really analyze this, you will find that focusing does not lead to doors being shut. Instead, a successful focus leads to new doors being opened. Surely, Carolina Klüft had no idea that she would one day be a successful TV presenter when she started competing in heptathlon.

A more meticulous reader may perhaps think, "Hm . . . this principle is about focusing, while the previous principle concerned being curious about change, the ability to challenge permanent things and test the limits. Isn't there a contradiction between, on the one hand, focusing and thus rejecting a multitude of opportunities and, on the other hand, encouraging curiosity about change?" Our response to this is: "No, we see no contradiction whatsoever between these two principles. Let's exemplify using Google."

Google's business idea is "to organize the world's information and make it universally accessible and useful." This is a pretty clear focus. Google is not involved in, for instance, travel operations or car manufacturing. But, the meticulous reader now counters, Google is developing self-driving cars! The reason for this is that due to its clear focus on making information available, Google has pondered a great deal regarding which areas will be the most important in the future. These thoughts have led Google to think outside the box and adopt a curious mindset as to which changes are on the horizon. This analysis, in turn, led to identifying self-driving cars as an area to focus on. If cars are to drive safely without human drivers, they need to collect and manage a large amount of information. Be sure that Google followed Jobs' recommendation to choose carefully when making the choice to focus on self-driving cars.

We believe that organizations that establish systematic processes that drive focusing will be successful and innovative over time.

2.1.4 Principle 4: Process Orientation

In "expert-based" organizations, there are people with answers to all questions facing the organization. Some tend to be experts in everything, even when it comes to things they have no expertise in whatsoever. Problem solving in this type of organization frequently involves these experts—people responsible for aspects such as quality, production technology and planning—deciding on how to address problems (or hiring consultants).

In a process-oriented organization, it is important to establish processes for how to address problems—processes that create a sense of safety in the organization. If you have a reliable process for managing a problem, then it is no longer a problem. By focusing on the process, more people can be invited to solve the problem. This creates engagement. Processes take time to introduce and they need to be maintained and developed. Hence, it often feels initially as if process-oriented organizations need more time to solve their problems. In the long run, however, this is a good investment.

> *We believe that established processes in a process-oriented organization eventually create quality-assured solutions that can be implemented quickly. Thereby, the problem-solving capabilities in expert-based organizations are quickly exceeded.*

Process orientation means toning down the focus on individuals. A process orientation means that you seek to optimize the process regardless of individual variation. A transformational form of leadership focuses on processes, while a transactional leadership blames (and rewards) the individual and the individual's actions. The difference between a transactional and transformational form of leadership is discussed further later.

According to Liker and Hoseus (2008), the word *problem* constituted one of the most significant challenges when Toyota was established in the United States. The reason was that "problem" in the West is frequently seen as something negative and linked to someone doing something wrong. It took some time for the managers at Toyota to realize this. Table 2.1 illustrates the cultural differences.

It may be obvious, but we still say it: process orientation is closely linked to a standardized working method à la Toyota. Of course, this foundation for lean management also applies when we discuss Hoshin Kanri. Without a standardized working method, it is not possible to compare the results of the process. And without comparisons, it is not possible to improve the process. In a process-oriented organization, it is understood that you analyze and document the way you work in order to establish a standard.

Standardizing the way you work may not sound like much fun. It may seem that it would stifle your creativity. However, this concept does not concern standardization in a Taylorist sense of the word, where the aim was to streamline mass production and enable clearer monitoring and control. This is not the purpose of standardizing working methods in Hoshin Kanri or lean management. At least not if you listen to a guru in lean:

> As we will see, standardized work was never intended by Toyota to be a management tool to be imposed coercively on

> the work force. On the contrary, rather than enforcing rigid standards that can make jobs routine and degrading, standardized work is the basis for empowering workers and innovation in the work place.
>
> **(Liker 2004 p. 142)**

When we ask the participants in our courses how their strategy process is designed and whether it is standardized in one way or another, a surprising number of participants say no. Our impression is that strategy work is rarely in focus when organizations engage in development efforts. So, imagine the kind of success you can achieve with quality-assured strategy work! Perhaps you should start with a survey of your current strategy work to enable you to continuously create increasingly successful strategies. At Lindbäcks Bygg, they realized that quality-assured strategy work was crucial for their growth (see Box 2.3).

Table 2.1 What Is a "Problem"?

	Western perspective	*Toyota*
What is a problem?	The result of someone having done something wrong	A deviation from the accepted standard
What is the reason?	The individual	The system
Who is responsible?	The person who made the mistake	Management
What should the person having made the mistake do?	If possible, solve the problem by themselves	Point it out and help prevent the problem from reoccurring
Perspective on human nature	People don't accept blame unless forced to do so by management	People are strengthened by receiving positive feedback for having identified a problem
Problem-solving skills	Some have them, others don't	They can and must be taught

Source: Freely based on Liker and Hoseus (2008 p. 166).

BOX 2.3 KNOWING WHERE YOU ARE AND WHERE YOU'RE HEADED

Stefan Lindbäck, CEO of Lindbäcks Bygg, says:

> My father and I have completely different abilities. He was incredibly successful in taking the company to where it was in 2011. But his problem was that he was a little bit too good! Everyone turned to him with all kinds of questions. He had all the answers. This doesn't work when you grow at the rate we are currently growing. I think we were very fortunate to have switched CEO when we did. I don't have the same abilities as he does, but I have other abilities that are very beneficial when growing and taking off. We are now like a full-grown company knowing where we are and where we are going for the next five years. This makes it much easier to embark on this journey and grow together. Everyone understands why we are making certain decisions this year, as this will result in something two or three years down the line.

2.1.5 Principle 5: Visualization

Visualization means making the organization transparent so that everyone understands their own role and the context in which they work. In Chapter 1, we mentioned that transparency and inclusion represent characteristics of an open strategy. Transparency occurs when you visualize the strategy for others. Visualization leads to engagement and enables inclusion and joint learning. In some organizations, the "experts" don't want to share their knowledge, or perhaps management thinks that the strategy should be secret. This may be a question of power based on the familiar adage that knowledge is power. Or it concerns the feeling of being chosen, being important, such as "I know something you don't."

Visualization is based on the opposite approach: inviting employees to participate in strategy work leads to better decisions and an even better execution. If management invites the employees by visualizing the way they think, this creates an example so that employees also visualize to each other. In turn, this creates an inclusive and engaging environment.

> *We believe that visualizing challenges and supporting inclusion represent a prerequisite for all members of the organization when engaging in strategy work.*

2.1.6 Principle 6: Managing by Learning

The traditional view of leadership concerns distributing work and monitoring how it is executed. However, Hoshin Kanri is based on the notion that the most important element is to develop the employees who will perform the work. The notion is that an organization's only unique competitive advantage is its people. Hence, one of the most important tasks for the leader is to develop and challenge the employees so that both the leader and the employees learn more. The leader thus becomes a coach helping the employees address their

BOX 2.4 LAISSEZ-FAIRE, TRANSACTIONAL AND TRANSFORMATIONAL LEADERSHIP

The leadership literature is a jungle. However, much of what is now being published is based on the ideas of Bruce Avolio and Bernard Bass[4] at the beginning of the 1990s. They argued that it is possible to distinguish between three leadership styles: laissez-faire, transactional and transformational leadership.

The laissez-faire style means that the leader in practice abdicates from their leadership role and lets the employees do what they want (*laissez-faire* is French and roughly means "let do").

Transactional leadership focuses on the transaction between the leader and the employee. In practice, the leader manages by means of rewards and punishments (carrot and stick). By clarifying expectations and conditions for employees and then carefully following up on their performance, it is possible to hand out punishments and rewards.

Transformational leadership is long term in nature. In this leadership style, the goal is for employees to develop so that they may lead themselves. This is achieved by the leader serving as a role model, communicating a clear vision, seeing and coaching the entire individual, offering intellectual stimulation (identifying interesting challenges) and having high expectations.

challenges. They seek to avoid solving the challenges themselves, as this will not develop the employees. Basically, this is a commitment to transformational leadership—a form of leadership placing the organization and its employees at center stage and looking upon the long-term learning of employees as more important than immediately solving current problems.

> *We believe that a leader focusing on learning and seeking to develop their employees and making themselves redundant will in the long run be a successful leader.*

2.1.7 Principle 7: Facts Drive and Decide

In Hoshin Kanri, facts serve as the point of departure. Facts are important in several ways. They are a fundamental starting point for developing experiments addressing clear and well-defined challenges. Without facts, the analysis of the current condition turns into guessing, thus making it impossible to effectively evaluate the result. To paraphrase *Alice in Wonderland*, it doesn't matter which path you take or where you want to go if you don't know where you are when your journey begins. Without a fact-based description of the current condition, you can't prioritize challenges or evaluate your actions. However, you must not lose sight of the objective.

Just as there are organizations where facts are not seen as valuable, there are organizations and individuals placing too much value on facts. It is not uncommon to find people who like to dig a little more in order to develop the analysis of the current condition instead of taking the next step and addressing the challenge at hand. Sometimes, one may suspect that this preference for further analysis is a way of avoiding other difficult steps, such as making decisions.

Nor should we forget that there are two objectives with regard to the analysis of the current condition. The obvious objective is to describe the current condition to a sufficient extent. The second objective is to create consensus with regard to this description. If you do not agree with the analysis on the current condition, analyzing even further will not be helpful.

The consensus objective highlights another problematic aspect, namely that descriptions of the current condition not based on facts can easily be called into question as subjective and not credible. If the description of the current condition is questioned, it will be quite some time until it is possible to address the challenge. That is why it is important to involve several people in the analysis of the current condition. After all, the people working on the challenge are the ones who decide what constitutes facts and what constitutes enough facts.

BOX 2.5 FACTS AS A METHOD FOR SOLVING PROBLEMS

At a company we visited, one of the managers said:

> Sure, we sometimes disagree within the management team. The fact that there are different points of view is a good thing. However, there also needs to be a problem-solving method—a method we have agreed upon to apply when we disagree. In our company, this method is called "facts." Find out the facts and we'll see who is right! This is often a question of us together taking a look at how the process takes place in reality. A well-known methodology in lean philosophy.

We believe that organizations placing a high value on facts are in a better position to address the right challenges in the right way.

2.1.8 Summary of the Seven Principles

At this stage, it should be clear that the seven principles overlap and simultaneously support each other. Unless you are driven by these seven principles, you can work as much as you like with Hoshin-inspired tools without success. When analyzing the working methods of an organization, we thus recommend that you go deep and try to capture how people work in the organization; in other words, you don't simply check off which analytical tools are applied; you also find out which principles actually drive the work. This is a difficult piece of advice, as it takes more time and requires a more in-depth analysis in order to evaluate the organization. However, this represents time and efforts well spent. By engaging in a principle-based analysis of the current condition, the result will be accurate and based on facts. This analysis thus offers a better basis for taking the next step. When you then use these principles and formulate your own visionary target condition for the strategy work, this will be unique.

Regardless of what the target condition will look like in your organization, it is important to keep two things in mind. One is that you do not contradict the principles. You can choose not to join (or, putting it differently, not to follow a particular principle), but if you contradict one or more principles, the overall logic is disturbed. The second thing to keep in mind is to be as honest

BOX 2.6 WHAT IS YOUR ACTUAL TARGET CONDITION?

Annika Sörenstam[5] was very successful already as a junior golfer. She wanted to win and frequently did so. After some time, however, a pattern started to emerge. She was clearly winning until she approached the end of the competition, when she suddenly dropped a few strokes and finished in second or third place. There was no denying the fact that she was in it to win, but why did she let herself lose her first position? Her father figured out why. She wanted to win, but she didn't want to be a winner! Why? Well, because a winner needs to address the audience and Sörenstam was so shy that she had absolutely no intention of speaking in front of everyone attending the competition. In other words, Sörenstam had a visionary target condition as a winner, something she actually did not want to achieve. She was not entirely honest with herself.

There are several ways of addressing this paradox. Sörenstam's father picked an approach that was somewhat of a gamble. He asked the organizers of several competitions to introduce a rule that the competitors ending up first, second and third should all have to make speeches. All of a sudden, losing the first place was not helpful. She started winning instead.

as possible with yourself. Does the organization really want to reach the target condition you are outlining? We discuss this line of reasoning in more depth in the next chapter when we analyze the current condition. However, at this point we choose to illustrate these ideas by using a quite familiar story (see Box 2.6).

The moral is that it is easy to formulate a visionary target condition that feels good at the moment, such as "We will double our sales in three years" or "I'm going to be a millionaire by the time I turn 30." But what does that actually mean? Why should we double our sales? Why do I want to be rich? And do the necessary sacrifices match the answer to that question? The same applies to Hoshin Kanri. Unless the visionary target condition for introducing the working method at hand is genuine, there will be no engagement, resulting in the organization not being prepared to make the necessary sacrifices.

2.2 A Scientific Approach

Just like lean management, Hoshin Kanri is based on a scientific approach. You start by analyzing a problem and formulating a hypothesis as to what caused the problem. This is followed by designing experiments to determine whether the hypothesis is correct. Once this has been decided, you may continue, either by formulating a new hypothesis if the first one was incorrect or by verifying the hypothesis and altering current working methods.

In theory, the scientific approach is quite self-evident. Unfortunately, however, it seems to be practiced less frequently. Next, we have listed four assumptions forming the basis of this systematic approach. You will find that there are several links between these assumptions and the seven principles presented earlier.

The *first assumption* is that it is a good idea to find out which direction to go before you start running. Careful consideration pays off in the long run. This principle should be obvious. Nevertheless, we time and again start running without thinking ahead. There are unfortunately quite a lot of us who open the package, put the instruction aside and start experimenting with assembling the Billy[6] bookshelf, or whatever the case may be. This is frequently based on some kind of macho attitude, because how difficult could it possibly be? Some people are successful using this strategy. They have a special talent. Most people, however, would benefit from a little more careful consideration.

This leads us to the *second assumption* in the scientific approach, namely that experiments represent a way of learning. The term experiment should be interpreted as something systematic and planned. In a scientific experiment, all assumptions are clearly outlined before the experiment begins (i.e., thinking before carrying it out). Otherwise, it is not possible to evaluate the experiment and you can't learn. However, this should concern experiments that are limited in scope, as the cost will not be all that high in the event of failure. If the experiment is small and planned, you can also easily analyze what went right and what went wrong. This means that it is easy to learn something from these experiments, regardless of whether it was successful. Perhaps the assumptions were spot on and only a small, easily corrected mistake ruined the entire experiment? Engaging in systematic experimentation means that you don't throw the baby out with the bathwater.

The *third assumption* is that the scientific approach benefits from a supportive working process. Everyone having worked with lean thinking will recognize the PDCA cycle (see Box 2.8). However, we have identified surprisingly few who have engaged in this working process in depth. A common problem is taking shortcuts, as you believe that you have understood the problem and seen the solution before you have access to an overall

BOX 2.7 RESPECT FOR PEOPLE

After reading in Chapter 1 about Gallup's study on levels of engagement in the private sector, one may question whether engagement is as important as we argue. If this were the case, surely more organizations would work more actively on this issue? Perhaps the book *Respect for People* by Kusén and Ljung (2015) may restore your faith in engagement. Robert Kusén's journey from the assembly line at heavy truck manufacturer Scania to being a successful consultant is both colorful and credible. His career is characterized by a view of people as having an immense number of resources. What determines whether these resources are used depends on the system at hand. If we create a working method that engages people, the employee will be engaged—and vice versa. This approach entails that those who create the working method, system, structures or leadership style are responsible for ensuring that there is engagement. In other words, the buck stops at top management. This is a radical notion when it is so much easier to blame the "inherent laziness" of employees—something that happens all too frequently.

BOX 2.8 PDCA—A SIMPLE AND COMPLEX TOOL

PDCA is both simple and complex at the same time. PDCA is an acronym for plan, do, check, act and it simply means that you should consider what to do before you do it and plan your activity in a way enabling it to be followed up (check) and that the results can be used throughout the organization (act). This was the simple part. The complex part relates to creating a culture in which it comes naturally to spend a lot of time analyzing the current condition, formulating objectives and identifying activities in the "P" part—activities that are then executed (do) and systematically followed up in order to learn something (check and act). In the following chapters, we return to the PDCA tool and the culture of systematic scientific analysis forming the basis of this tool. We discuss PDCA in more detail in Section 7.3.

picture. In the following chapters, we apply all the steps in the PDCA methodology to ensure the best possible end result.

The *fourth assumption* is that engagement beats everything. There are countless examples of organizations where some "strategist" has developed a great strategy that did not gain acceptance since there was no engagement in the organization. Engagement is created through participation, inclusion and an understanding of why the identified challenges are important. Later in this book, we discuss factors that determine the type of challenge to focus on. However, the most important factor is that the challenge should engage people.

The importance of the scientific approach cannot be underestimated. In a 1999 scientific study, Spear and Bowen argued that the scientific approach as expressed through the PDCA tool created "a community of scientists" at Toyota. According to these authors, the scientific approach and the working method it resulted in formed a key element in the Toyota culture.

BOX 2.9 WANT TO LEARN MORE?

A good guide on how to approach vision is the article by Collins and Porras. It is not new, but it is good!

- Collins, J. C. & Porras, J. I. (1996), Building your company's vision. *Harvard Business Review*, *74*(5), p. 65–77.

Want to learn more about 3M? There are many interesting texts available, but these two articles could be a good starting point.

- Coyne, W. E. (2001), How 3M innovates for long-term growth. *Research-Technology Management*, *44*(2), p. 21–24.
- Angle, H. L., Manz, C. C. & Van de Ven, A. H. (1985), Integrating human resource management and corporate strategy: A preview of the 3M story. *Human Resource Management*, *24*(1), p. 51–68.

A classic book on process management is:

- Harrington, H. J. (1991). *Business Process Improvement: The Breakthrough Strategy for Total Quality, Productivity, and Competitiveness*. New York: McGraw-Hill.

If you want to learn more about leadership, there is a lot to choose from. We recommend this book to start with:

- Jackson, B. & Parry, K. (2011), *A Very Short Fairly Interesting and Reasonably Cheap Book about Studying Leadership*. Thousand Oaks: Sage.

Many articles and books analyze Toyota's production system. One example is Spear and Bowen, who in an informative manner illustrate how this production system is linked to a number of basic rules, including the scientific approach:

- Spear, S. & Bowen, H. K. (1999), Decoding the DNA of the Toyota production system. *Harvard Business Review*, 77(5), p. 96–106.

And, of course, if you are thinking about the links between the principles of Hoshin Kanri and lean management, you should read Jeffrey Liker's classic work:

- Liker, J. K. (2004), *The Toyota Way: 14 Management Principles from the World's Greatest Manufacturer*. New York: McGraw-Hill.

Leadership is about people. Believing in people's intrinsic qualities is a good starting point for great leadership. Earlier in this chapter, we discussed the link to engagement. A good book on this topic is:

- Kusén, R. & Ljung, A. (2015), *Respect for People: Lean Success Requires a New Outlook on People*. Köping: Prog i Köping.

Notes

1. Seven principles may sound like a small number. In his well-known 2004 book *The Toyota Way*, Jeffrey Liker describes 14 principles presenting Toyota with world-class power to change. All of these are important in a production perspective. However, focus plays an important role when engaging in strategy work, which is why we limit ourselves to seven principles.
2. https://en.wikipedia.org/wiki/William_L._McKnight, accessed November 21, 2019.
3. From Wikipedia: "[Klüft] was an Olympic Champion, having won the heptathlon title in 2004. She was also a three-time World and two-time European

heptathlon champion. She is the only athlete ever to win three consecutive world titles in the heptathlon (2003, 2005, 2007), and was unbeaten in 22 heptathlon and pentathlon competitions from 2002 to 2007, winning nine consecutive gold medals in major championships." https://en.wikipedia.org/wiki/Carolina_Kl%C3%BCft

4. Avoilio, B., & Bass, B. Developing potential across a full range of leadership. *Cases on Transactional and Transformational Leadership*, 2002.
5. Annika Sörenstam is regarded as one of the best female golfers in history, having won 90 international tournaments in her professional career.
6. From Wikipedia: "BILLY is a bookcase sold by the Swedish furniture company IKEA. It is sold in over 60 million units worldwide. Its popularity and global spread have led to its use as a barometer of relative worldwide price levels." https://en.wikipedia.org/wiki/Billy_(bookcase)

Chapter 3

Are You and Your Organization Ready?

In Chapter 2, we described the visionary target condition of Hoshin Kanri—the utopian condition in which the Hoshin Kanri methodology is fully introduced into an organization. We used the word "utopian" since the very foundation of lean management, and thus Hoshin Kanri as well, is that you are never finished. It is always possible to make continuous improvements.

In this chapter, we focus on the analysis of the current condition. Here, we need to start with a limitation that is important to keep in mind when reading the chapter: *the focus is on the strategy work*. Hence, the analysis only refers to a part of the focal organization's current conditions and is guided by a simple question: What does your strategy work currently look like?

But to make things a bit more difficult, we start by reflecting on *your* current condition. You, the reader of this book. What does your current condition look like? What drives you to work with strategy? Are you engaged? We then go on to describe a way of identifying the organization's current condition by using a so-called Readiness Analysis. Finally, we include a more extended comment on the present strategy work in the analyzed organization.

We recommend that you read this chapter carefully and reflect upon what you read. This allows you to answer the question of whether you have the desire and engagement to work with Hoshin Kanri.

DOI: 10.4324/9781003194811-3

3.1 Why, Why, Why, Why, Why?

"Five whys" is a basic tool in the lean toolbox. The point of this tool is to encourage careful consideration. By analyzing the challenge of identifying the root cause, you may also identify a long-term solution. If you fail to determine the root cause, chances are that the solution will be incorrect. As we pointed out in the previous chapter, careful consideration pays off! (Read more about the Five Whys tool in Chapter 7.)

We have frequently asked ourselves the question of why. Not least when writing this book. When doing so, we have frequently asked ourselves: why should anyone read this book? Which kind of reader truly benefits from Hoshin Kanri? Next, we list the answers we have arrived at. Do you recognize yourself? If so, we strongly recommend that you read on.

- This is a book for those who either work with or are interested in leading and managing organizations. You work with strategy in one way or another. You may be hired as a consultant to coach others. You may be an owner or employee who works as a leader or manager in an organization. But you can also be a student or a "regular employee" who wants to address your own situation.
- This is a book for those who believe that everyone in an organization, regardless of formal position, can develop and improve it. In other words, you don't need to be a CEO or manager to benefit from this book. Strategy is something we all work with. And we do so constantly.
- This is a book best suited to those who are open to reflecting on and experimenting with *their own* way of thinking and doing things. This may lead you to also challenge the way others think and behave, but that is not always the case. If you develop yourself, you also develop others.
- This is a book for those who believe in the inherent desire in people to develop and improve themselves and their lives. In some cases, the flame is burning somewhat less brightly, but deep inside there is always a small glow left that may be brought back to life.
- This is a book for those who are curious about their nature and like to reflect upon the effects of their curiosity.
- This is a book for those who believe in small steps and who are persistent. We believe that determination and a long-term perspective are needed for achieving genuine development.

The majority of the preceding bullets relate to individual characteristics and how you look upon other people. In our view, strategy work is largely about people and people's behavior. The approach we describe is based on the desire and ability to challenge both ourselves and others in terms of the way we think and behave in organizations. A core aspect of genuine strategy work is also about setting a good example, which means that you must be as willing to challenge yourself as you are interested in challenging others. Are you ready to challenge yourself?

So, what might an organization working with Hoshin Kanri look like? In Box 3.1, we offer an example of this.

BOX 3.1 HOSHIN KANRI AT K-PORT

We had a very nice study visit at the company K-Port. Mats, the CEO, first offered an entertaining account of the company's journey over the past few years, followed by showing us the factory. On our way through the factory, we passed the painting section, where a young woman was painting. Mats commentated on this with a somewhat surprised tone in his voice. One of us asked Mats why he was surprised. His answer surprised us all.

"Well, Marie is quite a new employee and she hasn't painted before. But one of our overall objectives this year is to make us less vulnerable to sick leave, so it's brilliant that the work team has taken the initiative to train more painters. This position often turns into a bottleneck when people are on sick leave. It will be interesting to hear more about their thinking at the next meeting."

When we reconvened, Mats then told us how K-Port worked with strategy. Briefly, the strategic management team each fall identifies a few key challenges for the coming year—challenges that need to be addressed if the company's long-term vision is to be achieved. This year, one of these challenges was "make us less vulnerable to sick leave." The team managers, together with their team members, then had to consider how to address the given challenge and which activities should be carried out. Once they had discussed this with management, they could get started.

Once a month, the work teams first met for their own strategy meeting. It was in one of these that Marie had suggested that she should learn how to paint. After this meeting, the team managers and other managers in the company met in the strategic management team to discuss what the teams had learned from the activities carried out and how they wanted to improve the work on addressing the challenges.

Mats told us that he and his brother, who was the head of marketing, had just been on vacation for a week, without the phone ringing a single time! But now that he was back, it would be exciting to meet the team leaders at the next strategy meeting and hear more about their thinking with regard to Marie's initiative. He concluded by pointing out that his role as CEO was not to control and approve various kinds of initiatives. There were many instances when he didn't know which approach was the best. Everyone in the company had embarked on a joint learning journey, and all initiatives, successful or unsuccessful, could offer lessons.

You now have a decision to make. Do you find what you have read about Hoshin Kanri interesting? Do you have the energy needed to bring about an introduction of Hoshin Kanri in your organization?

If the answer is yes to these two questions, we suggest that you create a folder called "HK Strategy Work." You then create the first document in the folder and name it "My Vision." Here, you write down what you want things to look like in your organization. Don't think too long before you write—write down your spontaneous thoughts and feel free to be a bit visionary. Shoot for the stars! Once you have written down your preliminary vision, continue reading the book. This will probably give you more inspiration and enable you to go back and develop the first version into a visionary target condition.

This is an important piece of advice. When we discussed process orientation as a principle in Section 2.1.4, we emphasized the need to describe the standardized working method. Throughout the book, we return to the need for documentation. In many organizations, however, there is too much documentation. The problem is that the wrong things are frequently documented. What is documented is often the outcome, such as a policy or instructions (and perhaps the vision). The reasoning behind this, which answers the question of what the policy actually aims to achieve and which considerations were made when it was created, is not documented. In addition, the way it was applied is typically not evaluated. Do we follow the policy, the instruction or whatever the case may be? This is not written down.

BOX 3.2 DOCUMENT IN ORDER TO LEARN

Over the past year, we have completed two courses in which we have tested and developed our concept. We decided already from the outset to clearly document the process. We made a "flowchart" for each course where we documented our reasoning. After each part, all participants from the project (three to four people each time) wrote an evaluation or reflection. We then held a digital meeting where we discussed our reflections.

Prior to the next part, we started off in our joint reflections and further developed the concept. This meant that prior to the second course we had a solid documentation from the first course as input. In this way, we organized a thorough learning process. It took some time, but it would have taken considerably more time if we hadn't done this. We would not have been able to make well-considered quality improvements, meaning that we would have had to carry out three or four courses to achieve the result we now achieved after the second course. As stated earlier, careful consideration pays off in the long run.

The result is that continuous learning is neglected. Once there is a high level of discontent with a policy, someone is forced to review it. That someone needs to start from the beginning and ask themselves why the policy was created before they start reviewing.

Documentation is thus crucial when working with Hoshin Kanri. If thoughts and decisions are undocumented, they are more difficult to challenge as misconceptions and logical traps are easier to hide. This is why throughout the text we describe how documentation can be done in clever ways. Clever refers to documenting the right things and doing so in a concise fashion. Our aim is to reduce the jungle of documents already found all too frequently in many organizations. A clever way to achieve this is to use A3s. More on this tool in Chapters 5 and 7.

But in order to establish a good habit, you have to start small, so feel free to create your first vision document already at this point.

Now, after you have taken your temperature, the time has come to take the temperature of your organization.

3.2 Readiness Analysis

The question in the title of this chapter, whether you and your organization are ready, is actually phrased incorrectly. All organizations look different and differ in terms of their distance to the visionary target condition we described in Chapter 2. Nor is the purpose of a Readiness Analysis to measure the distance to the visionary target condition. The purpose of such an analysis is rather to initiate a dialogue in the organization on what the visionary target condition of the strategy work should look like. And, subsequently, in which areas the organization has the greatest potential for development.

We suggest that after reading the chapter you carry out an initial intuitive Readiness Analysis of your strategy work, without talking to anyone else. Don't forget to document your analysis in your new folder. In this way, you will learn more about the tool. Next, carry out a new analysis involving more people. We return to how to do this at the end of the chapter.

The purpose of a Readiness Analysis is to assess the potential for changing the way in which the organization works with strategy. In practice, this need can be separated into the existing *desire* for change and the existing *capacity* for change (Figure 3.1).

As will become apparent when we discuss strategies in Chapter 4, this potential is expressed differently depending on the balance between desire and capacity. Our experience in small and medium-sized organizations is that desire is crucial. If there is no desire to develop, capacity does not matter.

This analysis focuses on the strategy work, but it can also be carried out in several various contexts. You can carry out the analysis yourself to analyze the current condition and assess at which level your organization is presently and then decide how to introduce Hoshin Kanri. You can also perform the analysis with a team within your organization, such as the management team. This means that the analysis also becomes a way of calibrating the team.

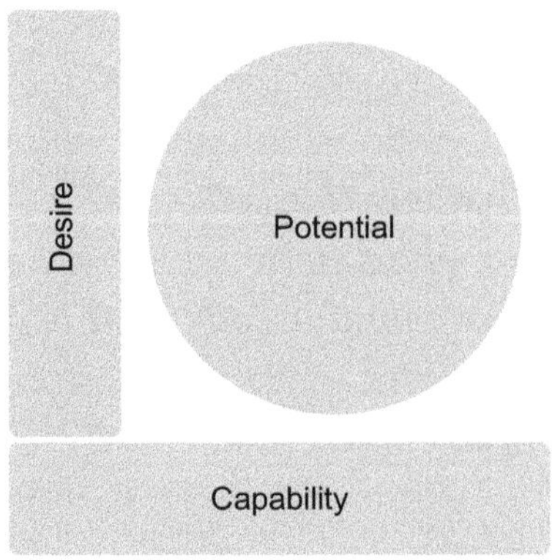

Figure 3.1 Desire and Capability Provide the Potential

What do the individual images and the team's joint image look like? But remember to be clear concerning the purpose and what is being analyzed.

Finally, a Readiness Analysis offers an opportunity to evaluate and learn. By performing such an analysis at the beginning, middle and end of a development project, you may initiate a good discussion on whether the development project has been successful and what you can learn from it.

We now discuss 12 factors in the Readiness Analysis according to which you can assess your organization's potential for development through its desire and capacity. To make this even clearer, we have also designed a checklist that you and your unit can use to rate your current condition (1–10). This checklist is designed so that the highest score is given to the organization fully living up to the visionary target condition described in Chapter 2. However, as we discussed earlier, you and the others in your unit may decide to use a different visionary target condition. In such a case, you will also need to redraft the checklist. We have supplemented the checklist with some explanatory text for each factor. (In Appendix 2, we present a worksheet that is easy to copy and use.)

Finally, we have included an example of a Readiness Analysis carried out by an organization participating in one of our courses.

3.2.1 External Drivers

Factor 1: External Pressure for Change

Is the organization successful in terms of profitability, achieving budgets and/or objectives? Is it possible to work with change efforts in a well-considered and long-term fashion? If so, is this a sign that the unit's internal and external efficiency is satisfactory (i.e., there are no obvious major problems that need to be addressed)? If profitability or achieving budget/objectives is not at a high level, is this due to external pressure to change? If so, does this pressure to change decide priorities within the organization and the pace at which you address your challenges?

This is an interesting item. Management might frequently perceive pressure for change as a nuisance while at the same time finding it difficult to define its exact scope and origins. If you are classified in the category of *low*, this indicates that the owners/managers of the organization are clearly dissatisfied with current performance and require swift results. In such an environment, it is difficult to pursue long-term change efforts, such as

BOX 3.3 FACTOR 1: EXTERNAL PRESSURE FOR CHANGE

Low = 1	Medium = 5	High = 10	Points
An immediate pressure for change only allowing for short-term change efforts	No clear external pressure for change and/or unclear interpretation of such pressure	Clear pressure for change allowing for long-term development efforts	

introducing Hoshin Kanri. The category of *medium* indicates that you need to prioritize a thorough analysis of the organization's current condition before proceeding with introducing Hoshin Kanri. The category of *high* indicates a good starting point for introducing Hoshin Kanri. In such a situation, there is consensus on what the pressure for change looks like, as it is clear, while there is also room for working with long-term improvements.

Factor 2: Ownership Control

Ownership governance and control is frequently discussed in the business context. But the topic makes sense in other organizations as well, when you reflect upon the relationship between those who manage a unit, department or project and those paying—their owners! Is there a clear link between the overall objectives of the organization and how the unit is managed? Is the distribution of governance roles clear? Are there conflicts of interest among owners? Are there clear arenas (steering group, board, etc.) for addressing possible management issues? Does there exist a written ownership directive in which the owner's long-term objectives are clearly stated?

In the previous chapter, we mentioned laissez-faire leadership, and this leadership style dominates the category of *low* with regard to ownership control. This is problematic when you want to develop your strategy work and introduce Hoshin Kanri, as this approach is based on clear expectations as to what should be achieved. If the owner does not communicate such an expectation, it needs to be identified by the management team. Is management interested in this? Or is it simply "fat and lazy"? If you find yourself in this category, there is thus a great need to improve the dialogue

BOX 3.4 FACTOR 2: OWNERSHIP CONTROL

Low = 1	Medium = 5	High = 10	Points
Nonexistent or ad hoc governance	Distinct owners, but a lack of clarity in governance intentions	Clear, long-term ownership control offering support and adding expertise There exists a written owner directive	

with the owners. In the *medium* category, there is a need to initiate a more systematic dialogue with the owner. In the *high* category, there is clear support for the Hoshin Kanri approach in terms of the owner's expectations or a driven management team that takes responsibility for its own ownership control.

3.2.2 Internal Drivers

Factor 3: Level of Ambition

Is the general feeling that you are satisfied with the current state of your organization? Or is there a constant drive to develop and improve? If there are no immediate challenges to address, do you create your own "challenges" within the organization?

A *low* level of ambition is often linked to the laissez-faire mentality among the owners described in Factor 2. If there are no performance requirements, there will typically not be any performance. In such a case, there is also no incentive to change things by, for example, introducing Hoshin Kanri, which presupposes high and clear ambitions. If you find yourself in this category, you should consider doing something other than developing strategy work, as this is an uphill battle. Just as mentioned previously, the *medium* category indicates that perceptions need to be clarified before proceeding with the introduction. A *high* level of ambition indicates that there is a documented ambition that is also communicated in the organization. This is an excellent starting point for introducing Hoshin Kanri.

BOX 3.5 FACTOR 3: LEVEL OF AMBITION

Low = 1	Medium = 5	High = 10	Points
Consensus on being satisfied with the state of affairs	Unclear and at times differing opinions as to whether things are satisfactory	The organization is driven by a clear ambition to develop and improve	

Factor 4: Focus

Focus can be short term, long term or, preferably, a combination of the two. Focus may be directed internally to improve internal efficiency by streamlining internal processes, thus resulting in cost savings. The focus can also be directed externally to create external efficiency (e.g., by developing goods/services that customers are willing to pay more for or simply selling current goods and services at a higher price). What is your focus? And how focused is your focus?

Our impression is that many organizations (management teams in particular) have not carefully considered their focus. The agenda in meetings mostly consists of information and is otherwise driven by events. In other words, many organizations find themselves in the category of *low*. In the *medium* category, there is an awareness of what you focus on but perhaps not a well-considered justification for why things look the way they do. *High*, well, we don't really need to comment on this level.

BOX 3.6 FACTOR 4: FOCUS

Low = 1	Medium = 5	High = 10	Points
No focus	Internal or external focus Clear long-term or short-term development efforts	Balanced internal and external development efforts Well-balanced short- and long-term projects	

Factor 5: Leadership

As we noted in Chapter 2, the company might engage in transactional leadership, meaning that the leader looks for deviations from rules and standards. When this occurs, rewards or punishments are handed out. The assumption is that the employee is driven by clear material rewards and punishments, which is why it is important to be clear about conditions, how behaviors are evaluated and the relationship to rewards (and punishments). If there are no clear standards from which there may be deviations, the leadership will be ad hoc based, unclear and ill conceived.

Transformational leadership can be described in terms of pride, respect, trust, communication, common sense, coaching and individual adaptation. The point of departure is that the leader assists in creating meaning in the work by clearly linking activities to an overall objective, which will lead to the employee being motivated and enthusiastic in their work. What is the dominant leadership style in your organization?

In the previous paragraph, we wrote "dominant leadership style." This indicates that this analysis is broader than exclusively applying to the style of the CEO or COO. Depending on the unit of analysis, this involves top management or a substantial number of additional individuals. In the category of *low*, we have lumped together ad hoc leadership and the laissez-faire style. In both of these, the point is the lack of a clear leadership style. Most organizations combine transactional and transformational leadership. In the *medium* category, however, transaction-based leadership dominates, where performance is in focus. In the category of *high*, it is clear that individual development is the number one priority, based on the assumption that if the individual develops, this will improve performance.

BOX 3.7 FACTOR 5: LEADERSHIP

Low = 1	Medium = 5	High = 10	Points
Focus on putting out fires Ad hoc–based or absent leadership	Clear transactional leadership	Transformational leadership Encouraging/ coaching and communicating	

We have noticed that there is a desirable leadership style in many organizations, a desired style that is not always in harmony with the practiced leadership style. The desired leadership style is often described in various policy documents related to leadership development/training or when recruiting managers. These descriptions may offer a good, neutral point of departure for discussing this issue (e.g., in your management team). Do you practice what you preach?

Factor 6: Management Work

Is there a management team in your organization? Does it have regular meetings? Are there clear roles in the team? Are these meetings recorded? Are decisions regularly followed up? Are managers in the team representing their function or (together) managing the organization?

Are there development efforts and/or learning focusing on the working methods (e.g., by rotating the role of chairperson)?

A typical Hoshin Kanri question is: "Why is there a management team?" This question may at first glance appear silly, but it is not, as there is no obvious answer. In many management teams, the main purpose is for functional managers to inform the CEO or COO on what is going on and get their approval and comments. Gathering functional managers all at once is rational for the COO, but this is not always the case for the functional managers. At the other end, we find management teams in which the functional managers balance the responsibility for their function with a responsibility for the overall direction. In such a situation, the management team becomes a resource for developing the organization. Obviously, this can also be linked to the types of issues being discussed. Is the agenda dominated by following up operational issues or by open, strategic, forward-looking issues?

In the *low* category, the management team serves no real purpose. If there is a formalized team to begin with, it rarely meets and the meetings are poorly planned. In the most common category, *medium*, the management team meets regularly and an agenda is communicated prior to the meetings—frequently the same for all meetings. Here, the focus is on information and control, mixing day-to-day and strategic issues. The participants tend to keep an eye on their respective turfs. In the category of *high*, the management team is focused on strategic issues. The group is well informed with regard to each other's functions and challenges. Information-sharing activities are minimized, as all are informed beforehand. The focus is on prioritizing and determining the conditions for how the prioritized issues

BOX 3.8 FACTOR 6: MANAGEMENT WORK

Low = 1	Medium = 5	High = 10	Points
No management team or team has irregular meetings Focus in meetings is on day-to-day operations	Management team exists, but meetings focus on information and operational issues Limited number of discussions on strategy One or a few individuals dominate meetings	Established management team Regular meetings and clear responsibilities Open discussions with a focus on development Members together manage the organization	

should be processed in the organization (who is responsible, when reporting should be carried out, and so on).

Factor 7: Strategy Work

Is there a systematic approach with regard to how the organization works with strategy? Are only a few or more people involved in the strategy work? Is the strategy documented? Is it followed up? Is there a systematic approach for developing the strategy work? Someone assigned responsibility for this process? In practice, do one or more people decide upon strategic issues?

Many of the smaller organizations we have studied fall into the *low* category. This is not surprising, as all organizations are to some extent caught up in their history. In these smaller organizations, the entrepreneur who launched the organization still owns and manages it. They started by making all the decisions concerning the organization and continue to do so out of habit. Somewhat larger organizations (but also truly large ones) often end up in the *middle* category. Someone has recognized the need to more clearly improve the strategy work and include more people, but there is no perseverance. Strategy work is done on an ad hoc basis, frequently with the help of a consultant and with a focus on analyzing and choosing strategy, after which it is quickly forgotten. The plan often ends up in some drawer.

BOX 3.9 FACTOR 7: STRATEGY WORK

Low = 1	Medium = 5	High = 10	Points
Nonexistent strategy work or in the hands of one or a few individuals No follow-up regular strategy work. No transparency, inclusiveness, or follow-up	No regular strategy work focused on analyzing and the formulation of a strategic plan When appearing the focus is on formulating a strategic plan	Systematic and recurring strategy work Several people involved Continuous follow-up with a focus on learning	

In order to qualify for the category of *high*, strategy work must include a broad range of employees. Above all, however, the strategy must be implemented and followed up. If there is no follow-up of the strategy, there is no point in having one. If you then take the time to reflect upon the process and learn something for next year, then it's a ten pointer.

Factor 8: Problem Solving

Is there a systematic approach to how problems are prioritized? Is there a methodology for solving problems? Are emerging problems seen in your organization as a threat or as an opportunity for making improvements? Is the manager the "firefighter" or are several or perhaps all employees involved in problem-solving activities?

All organizations encounter problems. It is frequently said in lean management that an organization without problems has a major problem! But how do we solve these problems? In the *low* category, the manager is the one solving problems. That is why the phone of the CEO or COO is almost constantly ringing and why the manager can never really take any time off. In such a system, the manager ends up being a bottleneck, and it goes without saying that the problem-solving approach becomes reactive. In the *medium* category, there is often an awareness of how problems should be solved in the organization (e.g., an escalation ladder). In practice, however, this is not fully adhered to. Once an organization has reached the category of *high*, there is

BOX 3.10 FACTOR 8: PROBLEM SOLVING

Low = 1	Medium = 5	High = 10	Points
No systematic approach Primarily reactive ("putting out fires") The manager solves problems	Problems are often solved where they arise No clear methodology	Well-established methodology Follows a clear problem-solving process (e.g., PDCA) Many people are involved in solving problems	

an established problem-solving methodology used by everyone. Knowledge regarding the order of priorities and escalation is disseminated throughout the organization. We mention PDCA in the checklist as an example of a problem-solving methodology, and we return to this tool in Chapter 7.

Factor 9: Body of Knowledge

Where do you find knowledge to use when solving problems and/or developing your unit? Does "we/I know best" apply? Or "call the consultant"? Or do you say, "Let's sit down together and get a handle on this problem so that we may then decide whether we ourselves know what to do or whether we need to call in someone from the outside"?

Knowledge is an interesting phenomenon. In organizations found in the *low* category, a few people know everything (or think they do)—one or a few "experts" possess the organization's core knowledge. This results in the organization becoming extremely dependent on these individuals. In the *medium* category, there are often one or more "bodies of knowledge." These may be individuals but may also be a formal documentation system where data is stored. Often there exist several parallel systems partially overlapping each other. The lack of a systematic approach with regard to knowledge generation makes it difficult to find relevant knowledge when needed. In practice, this means that you still rely on the knowledge of the experts. In the *high* category, the nature of the problem determines how to address the question of knowledge. Who owns the problem? What kind of internal knowledge exists that may be applied (past experiences)? How may

BOX 3.11 FACTOR 9: BODY OF KNOWLEDGE

Low = 1	Medium = 5	High = 10	Points
We ourselves know best	There is a body of knowledge but no systematic generation of knowledge	We find the answers through our problem-solving process There is a clear knowledge structure	

we supplement this internal knowledge? How do we systematize the new knowledge in our systematically created body of knowledge? If you have answers to these questions, then you qualify as a ten!

Factor 10: Visualization

Is information on how the organization is developing offered on a regular basis? Is the organization transparent in terms of both the information from management to employees and the information between employees and functions? Have you taken the next step and visualized the situation by regularly disseminating news, information, measurements and the like on message boards or monitors? Are there systematically organized daily management boards? Is there an established method for how you work with daily management?

An organization found in the *low* category is characterized by short-term optimization. The ambition is for employees to have precisely the knowledge required to perform their current tasks. All other information is unnecessary; it only complicates things. This is an environment with a very low level of visualization. An organization in the *middle* category has taken a big step. It clearly visualizes the day-to-day performance of the organization and it is possible to make comparisons. In order to move toward the *high* category, not only operational aspects but also strategic aspects need to be visualized. This is often sensitive as what is now being visualized is the responsibility of management. Not achieving strategic objectives may lead to uncomfortable questions at staff meetings. . . . When a high level of visualization has been achieved, it is frequently combined with a leadership style

BOX 3.12 FACTOR 10: VISUALIZATION

Low = 1	Medium = 5	High = 10	Points
No visualization	Daily management using boards	High degree of visualization: vision, strategic objectives, problem solving, daily management and more Clear link to vision and long-term objectives	

in which you are not afraid to talk about problems and have an ambition to engage in long-term learning.

Factor 11: Inclusion

Does everyone in the organization actively participate in your internal meetings? Is the decision-making process transparent and possible to influence? Are important decisions explained? Do all employees look upon this as something positive? Are there systematic improvement efforts to include more people?

In the category of *low*, the general view in the organization is that strategy work is something that management, the CEO or the owner take care of and nothing that the rest of the organization should care about or need to understand. Those with an ambition to get involved or who just want to get a better understanding face tough resistance. In the *medium* category, the level of engagement is also low. This may be a result of employees being included to some extent (e.g., in an initial brainstorming session on trends and challenges), but when priorities and decisions are to be made, management is silent. If the result is then communicated without any clear explanation, the level of engagement will be low. Employees are thus well informed but at the same time not involved in the development efforts. In the *high* category, there is clarity regarding the level of inclusion, the reason why inclusion looks the way it does and its purpose. In an organization classified as high, there are often several cross-functional strategic projects involving many employees from different levels in the hierarchy.

BOX 3.13 FACTOR 11: INCLUSION

Low = 1	Medium = 5	High = 10	Points
No inclusion Strategic decisions come as a surprise to many people	The decision-making process is often described by management, but there is limited interest in the organization to participate since the impression is that it is not possible to influence things	Regularly recurring meetings where all/many employees are invited to work with strategic issues Clarity in terms of how the individual contributes to the strategy work	

Factor 12: Individual Follow-Up

Are there regular routines for performance reviews? Are there clear and established ways of measuring (individual) performance? Is there a (clear) link between the overall objectives/strategy of the organization and the individual goals as determined in the performance review?

The reason for including this final factor is that all people are a little bit opportunistic. If there is no form of individual reward, the level of engagement will decline. In order to qualify for the category of *high*, the

BOX 3.14 FACTOR 12: INDIVIDUAL FOLLOW-UP

Low = 1	Medium = 5	High = 10	Points
There is no systematic individual follow-up	There is systematic individual follow-up, but the link to the organization's needs for development is unclear	Systematic individual follow-up with a clear link to the organization's overall objective/strategy	

transactional aspect (i.e., a functioning follow-up system at the individual level clearly linked to the reward system) needs to be combined with an inclusive, transforming organizational environment in which individuals are invited to contribute.

3.2.3 The Organization's Desire and Capacity

The points you have assigned to each of the previously mentioned 12 factors are an indication of what the situation looks like in terms of your organization's desire and capacity. We now summarize desire and capacity, after which we discuss the whole picture in more detail.

The first four factors—pressure for change, ownership control, level of ambition and focus—are linked to the *desire* to change. The other factors—leadership, management work, strategy work, problem solving, body of knowledge, visualization, inclusion and individual follow-up—are linked to the *capacity* to systematically work with strategy according to Hoshin Kanri.

After you enter the points for each factor, you can rate your business in a matrix roughly indicating the current condition (see Figure 3.2).

As we stated earlier, the important thing about performing a Readiness Analysis is not the number of points you get. The goal is to establish a point of departure for the development efforts. Furthermore, as we initially wrote,

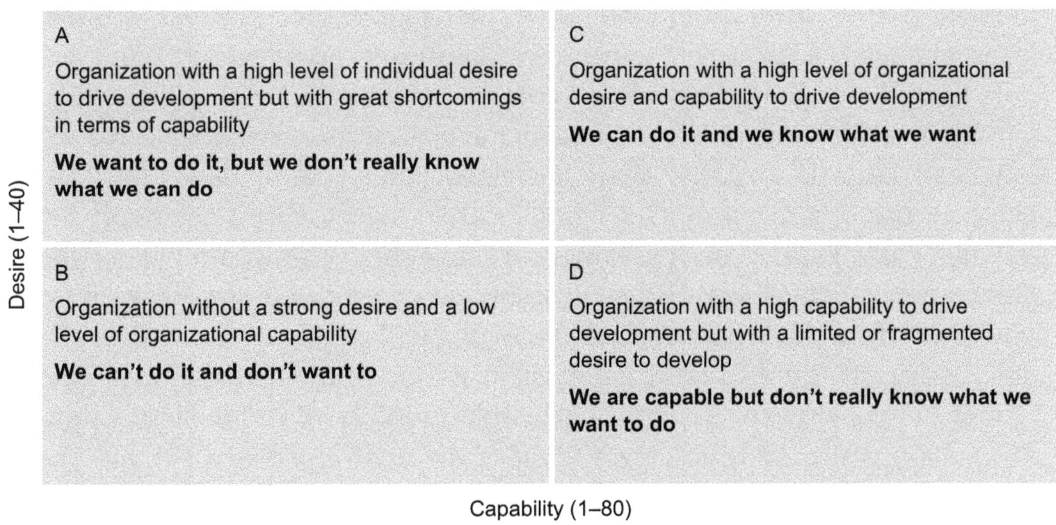

Figure 3.2 Classifying Organizations Based on Desire and Capability

the Readiness Analysis can be carried out in somewhat different ways and with different purposes in mind.

However, we suggest that you follow our advice and start by doing an analysis yourself. In the next step, as you widen the circle and include, for instance, the management team, this analysis may serve as a basis for a good discussion on what the joint current condition looks like. When you embark on this step, don't forget to apply an inclusive approach. *The aim is to create an interest in working further with the strategy development process, not determine which answer is right or wrong.* Interest and engagement can also be encouraged by not only filling out the checklist but also inviting others to develop the tool. Perhaps you can create your own organization-specific analytical tool based on the visionary target condition you have agreed on.

Box 3.15 describes a systematic Readiness Analysis carried out by an organization.

BOX 3.15 READINESS ANALYSIS IN PRACTICE

In this organization, they first chose to create a questionnaire answered individually by each member of the management team (A–H). The project manager then compiled the results (see Table 3.1). In total, the organization received an average of 26 plus 48 points, which would rank the organization above average in terms of both desire and capacity. In the next step, the project manager analyzed the data. She then noted that the responses differed quite significantly. With regard to the factor of strategy work, one person entered three points while another member of the management team entered ten. However, there were significant differences in other factors as well (see the far right-hand column in the table).

When a meeting of the management team was convened, it turned out that the task was not altogether clear. Some had assessed the situation in the organization as a whole. Others had focused solely on the management team. This explained, for instance, the difference in the assessment of the level of visualization. Another discussion concerned the meaning of these factors. How, for example, to assess external pressure for change in a public organization? Is everyone in the management team aware of how ownership control takes place and how visible it is? A third discussion concerned the conclusions of the analysis. Based on this discussion, it was noted that even if they had ranked themselves fairly well in terms of strategy work, there were significant shortcomings in the field of visualization. Inclusion in the strategy work also needed to be prioritized.

Table 3.1 Results of the Readiness Analysis

		A	*B*	*C*	*D*	*E*	*F*	*G*	*H*	*Average*	*Diff.*
1	External pressure for change	4	8	3	5	7	5	5	3	**5**	5
2	Ownership control	7	5	7	7	5	8	7	5	**6**	3
3	Level of ambition	9	9	10	6	8	8	8	8	**8**	4
4	Focus	7	7	7	4	7	6	7	6	**6**	3
	Total Desire	**27**	**29**	**27**	**22**	**27**	**27**	**27**	**22**	**25**	**7**
5	Leadership	4	7	7	5	6	8	7	5	**6**	4
6	Management work	8	9	8	8	10	8	8	8	**8**	2
7	Strategy work	4	7	8	4	10	7	8	3	**6**	7
8	Problem solving	5	5	6	6	8	8	7	5	**6**	3
9	Body of knowledge	8	7	8	6	5	9	7	5	**7**	4
10	Visualization	2	2	8	1	7	2	5	1	**4**	7
11	Inclusion	3	3	5	5	7	3	7	5	**5**	4
12	Individual follow-up	2	5	6	7	8	7	7	3	**6**	6
	Total Capacity	**36**	**45**	**56**	**42**	**61**	**52**	**56**	**35**	**48**	**26**

Note: Dark shade: highest number (1:B, 2:F, 3:C, 4:A, 5:F, 6:E, 7:E, 8:E, 9:F, 10:C, 11:E, 12:e). Medium shade: lowest number (1:H, 2:B, 3: D, 4: D, 5:A, 6:A, 7:H, 8:A, 9:E, 10:D, 11:A, 12:A).

Don't forget to save the results and the different versions of the checklist. This creates a historical document, a form of documentation describing the "standard" for the strategy work process in your organization. This is an important function, since it is difficult to determine the change brought on as a result of the development efforts after the fact. If a Readiness Analysis is carried out once a year, you create a basis for reflecting and learning about the design of the change efforts.

Before we discuss change strategies in Chapter 4, there is a factor in the Readiness Analysis that we should focus some more on: factor 7, strategy work. Obviously, strategy work is the point of departure for the entire analysis. We have thus decided to conclude this chapter with a more in-depth discussion on the existing strategy work.

3.3 Existing Strategy Work

Most organizations already have experiences regarding strategy work. Perhaps there is an annual strategy process in place and existing ways of following up on objectives, such as (more or less) balanced scorecards.

The existence of an existing working method is often beneficial when you want to introduce Hoshin Kanri. For example, balanced scorecards and Hoshin Kanri have several things in common, thus enabling these methods to be successfully combined. Having an annual established strategy process could also mean that the organization has created a good sense of self-knowledge and developed objectives and visions shared in the organization. This is an excellent starting point for introducing Hoshin Kanri.

At the first stage, it is thus important to identify how the annual strategy process is conducted and has been conducted. If there is an existing strategy process or examples of attempts to structure and develop the strategy work in the organization, one may ask the following questions:

- Why was there an initiative to work systematically with strategy?
- Who took the initiative?
- Has it been repeated?
- Why was the initiative ended (if this was the case)?

If strategy work has been repeated or carried out on a regular basis:

- Has the approach been developed?
- Has the strategy work been evaluated?
- Is there any documentation?

Mapping and analyses based on these questions will help you recreate interesting and sometimes crucial knowledge in your organization—things that are so easily forgotten. It also gives you the opportunity to analyze the need for change and avoid some pitfalls in development efforts.

There are also some differences between Hoshin Kanri and more traditional approaches that can cause problems. We have noticed that there are times when a certain level of cynicism has materialized in relation to annual strategy processes. Some participate in the annual "rain dance" and primarily look upon it as a way of getting a break from the daily toil. Frequently, these participants have no faith that this work will result in anything tangible. This attitude is often combined with a clear division between the few people who develop the strategic plan (CEO, owner and perhaps management team) and the rest of the organization tasked with implementing it. If the follow-up of the plan is poor and the learning process from year to year is unclear, then it's easy for cynicism to flourish.

The point of departure in Hoshin Kanri is that many people should be included in developing strategy and that the division between those who develop and those who implement should be blurred. It may be difficult to receive engagement in this type of participation if many employees have a cynical perspective on strategy work.

Another "cultural" challenge is that Hoshin Kanri requires a strong drive for continuous learning. If the attitude is that everything has to work smoothly the first time it is implemented and that deviations are severely punished, it won't be easy to introduce a new approach to strategy, especially if the approach requires new ways of thinking and behaving. Another problems is that a learning perspective is sometimes confused with a need to be in control. The seemingly simple question "How is it going?" can be interpreted in many different ways. One interpretation is that it concerns checking whether the recipient has done what they were supposed to do. Another, more positive interpretation is that the person asking is interested in finding out how things are going in order to share experiences from the work, experiences that may improve the working method. We discuss "how to ask" in more depth when we discuss coaching techniques later in the book.

So far, we have mainly pointed out problems and pitfalls. In the following chapters, we are a little bit more positive and present solutions on how to introduce Hoshin Kanri.

BOX 3.16 THE SHELF WARMER

The research project on strategy work had just begun, and our aim was to understand how strategies arose in the participating companies. We were now to visit one of these companies for the first time and, as always, we asked a number of questions during the visit, all of which related to the 12 factors in the Readiness Analysis. When we came to the seventh factor in the analysis, strategy work, the CEO told us that they had carried out strategy work a few years ago. They had hired a consultant and brought together the top managers for a full day, focusing on strategy and values. "What was the result?" we wondered. The CEO proudly showed us a beautiful tapestry with the company's values in stitching. "But," the CEO reminded himself, "we also wrote a strategic plan . . . Hm, where did it go? It should be here in the bookshelf in the office . . ."

BOX 3.17 STRATEGY WORK AS A TEMPORARY PROJECT

A fictional account based on the experiences of several of the authors:

> We received an invitation to the annual strategy meeting well in advance. All 14 of us in the organization were invited, as usual. No requirement to prepare before we met. The meeting began by our CEO taking the floor and starting the day by saying, "Yes, the time has come for us to once again dust off our strategy." That didn't feel particularly engaging. He then presented the most important things we had arrived at the last time and presented an update on what had happened in the past year. We then worked in smaller groups. Our task was to evaluate the past year and consider whether the strategy needed to change. We had a good time and we worked well. It also turned into an interesting discussion when we reconvened. The CEO concluded by thanking us for our interest and explained that he had received very good input that he would integrate into the strategy. He would get back to all of us with a new version of the strategy. A few months have passed since then, and as far as I know, we have not been given an updated strategy. On the other hand, no one has asked for the update. We keep on working as usual.

BOX 3.18 WANT TO LEARN MORE?

Knowledge management is an interesting area. There is still much to learn in Ikujiro Nonaka's classic 1991 article. Nonaka shows how articulating quiet knowledge in organizations constitutes an important element of the development process. He also points out that knowledge is organic. We don't always know who needs which knowledge, which means that it is better to share knowledge with more people in the organization than what would seem necessary. This benefits innovation efforts, as innovations thrive when different unexpected skills are combined in new constellations. Read the latest version of Nonaka's article:

- Nonaka, I. & Takeuchi, H. (2007), The knowledge-creating company. *Harvard Business Review, 85*(7/8), p. 162–171.

As discussed earlier, the visualization factors in the Readiness Analysis are closely linked to the concepts of inclusion and transparency. An article by Hautz et al. discusses the possibilities and dilemmas that may result from inclusion and transparency:

- Hautz, J., Seidl, D. & Whittington, R. (2017), Open strategy: Dimensions, dilemmas, dynamics. *Long Range Planning, 50*(3), p. 298–309.

Chapter 4

Strategy for Introducing Hoshin Kanri

In Section 3.2.3, we used the results of the Readiness Analysis to place the analyzed organization in one of four possible boxes (A–D) according to the dimensions of desire and capacity. In this chapter, we first discuss this classification in more detail. We then discuss how to introduce Hoshin Kanri.

4.1 Classifying Organizations Based on Desire and Capacity

As previously discussed, desire and capacity are both important aspects when deciding on how to introduce Hoshin Kanri. But most important out of the two is desire. If the capacity is low, the introduction will only take longer. The lack of desire is more difficult to address. This difference is important to keep in mind when reading about the four categories, discussed next.

4.1.1 Category A: We Want to Do It, But We Don't Really Know What We Can Do

In this type of organization, powerful individuals have a strong desire and ambition to develop the organization (typically founder and/or owner). However, there are major shortcomings in terms of capacity, concerning moving from one or more individual desires to a clear organizational desire. This is an important point, because a great dependence on individuals

DOI: 10.4324/9781003194811-4

in the organization creates a "culture of experts," uncertainty and, subsequently, short-term action.

Our experience is that category A organizations have a long way to go in terms of introducing Hoshin Kanri. There is no point in building an organizational capacity before the various individuals have agreed on how to develop the organization as a whole. The first step in such a process is to establish a common platform enabling the individuals concerned to start talking to each other.

Box 4.1 illustrates the problem of being dependent on individuals and teams, while Box 4.2 presents an example of what may occur when individual desires can't reconciled.

BOX 4.1 BEING DEPENDENT ON INDIVIDUALS AND TEAMS

In 2015, Swedish sports newspaper *Sportbladet* published an article in which they presented goal statistics for the Swedish national soccer team. They noted that for five years, Sweden had scored 68 goals in 33 official games with other nations. When Zlatan Ibrahimović[1] was on the field, only six of these goals had been made by someone who started the game as a forward together with Zlatan. The article then discussed the reasons for this. What should happen was that Zlatan would attract defenders, thus opening up for the other forwards. The article suggested that Zlatan's expertise as someone scoring goals had made the Swedish team overly dependent on him. What happens when the expert no longer wants to play? So far things have worked themselves out pretty well. However, when I write this, it seems as if Zlatan is back in the national soccer team. I wonder if it will be a new game this time.

BOX 4.2 THE NONEXISTENT MANAGEMENT TEAM

It was the fourth workshop at the sawmill with 15 employees. As usual, the entire office was invited, meaning the four relatives, two of whom owned the business. Just as at the last meeting, only three made it. The fourth was on a business trip in Germany, something the other members of the team had not found out until the previous day. The first issue on the agenda was establishing a management team where the four were to be included. Unfortunately, they had not been able to arrange a meeting on their own since the last workshop. At least one of them was always unable to attend when the team was to meet. This had been the case for several months. After the workshop, the project management stopped working with the company. Obviously, there was no common interest in jointly developing the organization.

At this sawmill, we failed to create a common platform enabling the individuals to start talking to each other about the organization's long-term objectives. The management team was the intended platform for introducing Hoshin Kanri. We had also agreed with the CEO in terms of an important challenge that the management team could start experimenting with. Unfortunately, this was not enough, as the personal differences were so great that we had to end this collaboration.

4.1.2 Category B: We Can't Do It and Don't Want To

Category B organizations should not really be able to exist. There is no pronounced desire for development and the capacity is limited. However, many organizations fit into this category, and most of them do quite well. Owners or CEOs frequently point out that their competitiveness is based on their flexibility. In practice, this means that they do whatever enters their mind or, perhaps more frequently, that they do what the customers want them to do. The trick to survive is that management (typically owners of small companies) work long days without paying themselves a reasonable salary.

If you, the reader of this book, work in a category B organization, you are probably quite frustrated. The conditions for engaging in systematic strategy work in these organizations do not look good. One way of finding motivation and job satisfaction in this type of organization is to adopt a small-scale approach to development. If you are responsible for a department, section or other organizational unit, you can start systematizing your own strategy work there. Just like the Readiness Analysis, Hoshin Kanri can also be applied at different organizational levels or in different units. Who knows? If changing the way your unit operates is successful, it may turn into a wake-up call for the organization as a whole.

4.1.3 Category C: We Can Do It and We Know What We Want

Category C is broad in nature. There are organizations with clear, joint objectives because a strong-willed individual has determined that this should be the case and the rest of the organization has adapted accordingly. It is frequently challenging to introduce Hoshin Kanri in such cases, as the prevailing (often patriarchal) culture counteracts an increased inclusion of employees in the decision-making process. However, this category also includes organizations where the objectives have been developed and are "owned" by many individuals in the organization and where there is a strong collective culture of development. If the latter is linked to an organizational capacity to drive development, the organization is in a very good position to introduce Hoshin Kanri.

4.1.4 Category D: We Are Capable But Don't Really Know What We Want to Do

Category D is interesting. Here, it often concerns ambitious managers having prioritized internal efficiency (e.g., they already know how to work according to lean principles in their production). However, the same managers have not raised their gaze and started to look beyond the treetops. They have not realized the potential of the organization, which is why they have not started to think about what they (and their employees) can and want to achieve. These are fruitful organizations to develop. Once an understanding of the importance of working on strategic issues has been established and some tools have been introduced, things get moving, almost by themselves!

BOX 4.3 NEEDED FOR WHAT?

A CEO told us about the drastic consequences resulting from an apparently small redistribution of authority and responsibility in his company. This example is important as it illustrates a major change in the role of management (in this case, the role of the CEO). From being the fixer everyone depended on, he felt as if he was on the sideline and almost no longer needed:

> I always worked overtime during the weeks, and on the weekends, I got to fix what hadn't been done in production. This was unsustainable. A few months after we invited the employees to

actively take responsibility in their respective areas, all of a sudden no one came to me asking for help. It was almost a life crisis. I had nothing to do! Fortunately, I'm a trained electrician, so I got to work on rewiring the electricity in the factory. This kept me busy for three weeks.

4.2 Challenge-Based Change Strategy

After the Readiness Analysis, you need to make a decision in relation to two questions. The first question concerns whether to introduce the entire Hoshin Kanri annual planning cycle at once or whether to start with a challenge-based approach. And if you have chosen a challenge-based approach, how complex should the challenge be? The second question concerns the content, what the challenge should focus on. The annual planning cycle alternative is discussed in detail in Chapters 5 and 6, but even if you choose this option, we recommend that you read this chapter first, as the next section discusses such aspects as the role of the change agent.

If you choose to adopt a more incremental strategy for introducing Hoshin Kanri and thus work with a challenge-based approach, we recommend that you introduce Hoshin Kanri at a basic level if your organization is classified as category A or B. By this we mean that the work is limited to one or a few individuals in order to reduce the level of complexity. In other words, this involves concentrating on "low-hanging fruit" in order to achieve relatively quick results leading to engagement to carry on the work. Perhaps the entire management team is involved or only a few key individuals are selected. The more centralized the organization, the more important it is to include key individuals in the work.

So, how do you convince these key individuals? One way that we have heard is quite effective is to visit other organizations that have successfully introduced Hoshin Kanri, thereby creating an openness to change. Since it is difficult to directly link the introduction of Hoshin Kanri to a financial result, these study visits can clarify how "soft factors" such as engagement and inclusion affect the working environment and create motivation, which, in turn, bring about better results. The fact that others have done this can also spur the competitive spirit of key individuals. However, the aim should be to turn these study visits into *learning trips*. Many study visits are leisure trips, a nice break from the day-to-day work. A learning trip is carefully planned. What do you want to study? Why should you study this? How are you to document and evaluate the knowledge obtained? And how is it to be used? If you make a learning trip, you also need to offer opportunities to discuss this within the group. What do you want to achieve with regard to internal change during your learning trip? The absolutely most important element is that you don't forget what you have learned. Regularly refer back to important points from the learning trip. Turn the visit into a sort of compass for change. If you want a really good result, you should first make the same study visit alone so that you are prepared for all possible questions.

The next step is to receive study visits. The point of this is that when you are to present yourself to others, you are forced to learn your own organizational logic. When you do this, you frequently notice gaps in the logic, which can trigger a desire for change. But this is also a risky step. If the reception is a failure, you may be out of work the following day . . .

As we suggested earlier, our basic philosophy is that in organizations classified as categories A and B, it is crucial that you build engagement for developing—a driver. Our recipe for doing so is to be open to external impulses, such as study visits and learning trips. Those of us who run and have run development projects have encountered many examples of how the meeting between different organizations has inspired and created an interest in development.

Once an interest in development has been established, the next step is to identify a suitably complex challenge to use as a starting point. The time has now come to introduce the concept of "low-hanging fruit," as this is exactly what we mean when we refer to a suitably complex challenge. In other words, the challenge should offer a good opportunity to practice using important analytical tools (see Chapter 7). The focus should be on creating a common basis in the organization for how to solve problems, preferably according to the systematic scientific analysis we presented in Chapter 2. This also means that it is a good idea to introduce PDCA at an early stage, something we discuss in detail in the next chapter.

Introducing a tool without applying it is counterproductive. And in order to create engagement and interest, you must carefully choose the challenge to which the tool (PDCA analysis) is applied. The challenge must be important to those involved but also positively charged, meaning that solving it will have clear positive effects. It doesn't have to be a strategic issue for the entire organization, but the solution to the challenge should in some way represent a significant improvement. In other words, it doesn't have to be a problem directly related to financial gains (i.e., making or saving money). On the contrary, it may involve spending a lot of time and not earning anything in the short term.

We have had, in different contexts, the pleasure of working with Lars Diethelm, one of four partners in the growth consultant company Ahrens. At Ahrens, they work with the concept of *profanities*. They actively listen for profanities, believing that these express frustration. And frustration is a good starting point for a new business opportunity. The idea is that what is cursed by a potential customer offers a potential for business development (see Box 4.4). However, these ideas are equally useful in this context.

BOX 4.4 EMOTIONS, PROBLEMS AND OPPORTUNITIES

In a book,[2] Lars Diethelm and Michael Engström write:

> Our choice to use a strong word such as profanity is very conscious. When someone curses, it is often an expression of strong feelings, and strong feelings are often associated with major problems. If we manage to find these major problems as well as a good solution to these, there is a good chance that we will be richly rewarded.

So, if you follow the advice of Lars and Michael, you simply listen for profanities in your organization. Which problems tend to result in cursing? Perhaps these problems represent your low-hanging fruit?

In Boxes 4.5 and 4.6, we present two examples of strategic challenges. The first was a low-hanging fruit yielding rich returns in the continued Hoshin Kanri efforts. The second represents the opposite.

BOX 4.5 CUSTOMER COMPLAINTS: LOW-HANGING FRUIT IN CUSTOMER SATISFACTION

Here is what the CEO of a specialist carpentry company has to say:

> Our niche is and has always been specialist carpentry. We have a limited customer base and our products are quite pricey. Everything is special. Even the customers are special. We don't advertise in a traditional sense. The customers come to us. Word of mouth is crucial. This was obvious to me and my brother, and

we believed that it was obvious throughout the organization. Just over a year ago, we discovered that this was not the case. When we started introducing Hoshin Kanri, we decided to focus on a challenge we had been struggling with for a long time. Customer complaints are not fun to handle. They were never prioritized. Something was askew here, even though we tried to focus on this challenge time and again.

We understood why when we were to motivate our employees regarding the importance of getting a handle on our customer complaints. When everyone understood the link between our business model, customer complaint management, our reputation and future survival, things more or less worked themselves out. Everyone was motivated to work systematically with customer complaint management as we recognized the importance of delivering the highest quality also when addressing complaints.

Since then, the number of customer complaints has dropped drastically, and I would argue that the complaints we nevertheless receive are now being managed in such a way that our customers are frequently more satisfied after the complaint process than they would have been without the complaint! The staff is satisfied, we are satisfied and, most importantly, our reputation is constantly improving and we are approached by new customers.

Customer complaints have become the strategic challenge that taught us a way of jointly working with strategy. We have learned to use various analytical tools, while we have also created a sense of engagement enabling us to move forward and take on other challenges, perhaps formulating an overall vision for the company and its strategy work.

BOX 4.6 ORDER AND STRUCTURE

After several meetings at the manufacturing company, we had arrived at the stage when the management team had decided to give Hoshin Kanri a shot. This meant that we simply needed to choose a challenge that they would start working on. One of the members of the management team quickly took the floor and suggested that the challenge should be “order and structure" in the office. Everyone present accepted the suggestion, but it was clear that the level of enthusiasm was quite limited. However, the person having made the suggestion didn't back down, and we started to jointly analyze the challenge. After a week or two, it became clear that an ordered and structured office was not a challenge creating energy and engagement. Other challenges were much more engaging and urgent.

So, our message is that organizations found in category A or B must start at level 1 of Figure 4.1 when introducing Hoshin Kanri.

This figure is based on the model PDCA, which stands for plan (analyze and plan), do, check (follow up and evaluate) and act (standardize). The latter is thus the part of the process in which the results from the problem-solving process are to be integrated into a standard in the organization.

As you can see in the figure, the P for planning is smaller than DCA at the first level of the PDCA tool. The reason for this is to avoid initially spending too much time on planning and analyzing the challenge to instead spend time on experimenting. These experiments turn the process into an activity, hopefully leading to positive results. This creates engagement. The

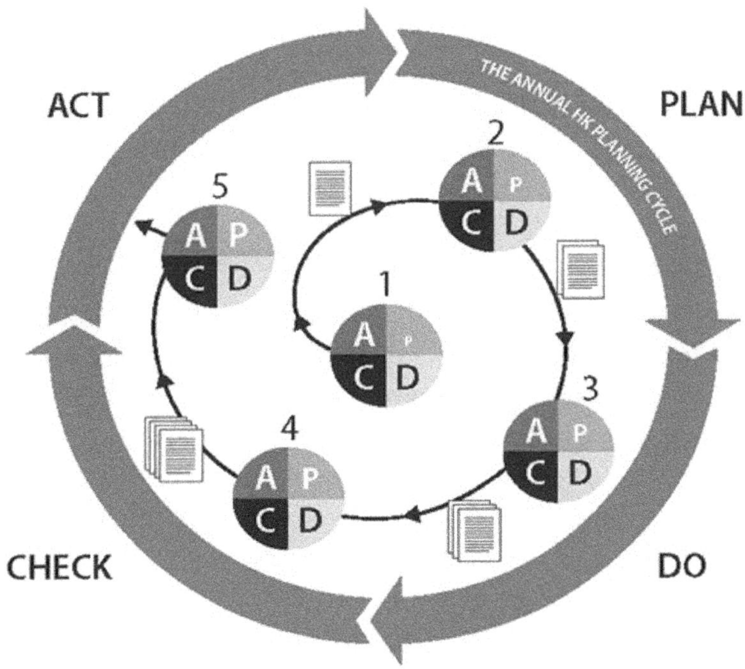

Figure 4.1 The Process of Introducing Hoshin Kanri

(Melander et al. 2016.)

outcome of the experiment also means that there is something to jointly reflect upon. If you do this, you may learn through the experiments. In Section 7.3, we describe what experiments refer to in the context of Hoshin Kanri, and this is something important to understand before initiating a challenge-based development project. Experimenting is about designing a mental learning trip, something that should be done with care.

It is important to allow time for reflection in the selected group (perhaps a part of the management team). Hopefully, this will create an increased level of engagement and a desire to move on to the next level, when additional time is allocated for analysis—and so on (see Figure 4.1, where the P in the PDCA model gradually grows in size). The growing pile of "sheets of paper with text" in the figure also illustrates that the amount of knowledge documented and shared gradually grows as challenges are added. If this documentation is well managed, it will be an essential part of the future annual Hoshin Kanri planning. Such documentation may take the form of, for instance, A3s (see Section 7.5.1).

As stated previously, organizations categorized as C or D are in a better position to introduce Hoshin Kanri. Hence, they can start later in the cycle (perhaps level 4 or level 5) and progress faster. Ideally, they can even start applying the Hoshin Kanri approach in its entirety already from the outset (i.e., the large annual cycle in the figure). (We present this strategy in Chapters 5 and 6).

Sometimes, things don't work out as planned. In Box 4.7, we describe our visit to a company we had categorized as a "good C company." We looked forward to working with them on a concrete and important challenge. Perhaps we would be able to start at level 4? Things didn't really turn out that way.

BOX 4.7 BELOW THE SURFACE . . .

We visited a manufacturing company with some 200 employees. They had a straightforward business plan clearly describing strategic challenges. Together with the management team, we decided to address one of these challenges. Before we got started, however, we asked some control questions. To our surprise, it turned out that the members of the management team did not have the same picture of the challenge. Consequently, their views differed in terms of how to address the challenge or follow up on the outcome. It turned out that the CEO "owned" the entire challenge, and he had not carried out any basic analysis of how it was to be understood or how it was linked to the company's vision. No wonder the work had ground to halt! The result was that we had to reverse the process and start the introduction at level 2 instead of level 4, as we initially intended. We had to put in a lot of work analyzing the current condition and establishing a joint picture of reality in the management team.

4.3 How Does the Change Agent Bring about Change?

In Section 3.1, we asked the basic question of whether you, our reader, are motivated to drive an introduction of Hoshin Kanri in your organization. Now that you have read an additional 30 or so pages and hopefully completed a Readiness Analysis, perhaps we can now refer to you as a change agent. It may thus be time to reflect a little on how the work of a change agent is carried out. To begin, we present Peter Häyhänen's account of how he worked with change at SÄS (see Box 4.8). His account is followed by some reflections.

BOX 4.8 PETER'S JOURNEY

Södra Älvsborgs sjukhus (SÄS) is a hospital with 3,900 employees and 410,000 visits in 2021. Peter Häyhänen is head of development at SÄS. He started working there in 2012 after a career at multinational telecom company Ericsson and multinational shipping company Maersk Line, where he worked with Six Sigma, lean and process development. Peter played an important role when redesigning the SÄS management work, and Hoshin Kanri represented an important element in this change. This is his account:

> I received my calling to work in healthcare in 1999 at a Six Sigma conference in Miami. I then realized that I wanted to work on making improvements for people and that there was great potential for developing the healthcare sector. When I left Maersk, I saw in the newspaper that the hospital director of SÄS at that time had started to introduce lean, that he was carrying out training with the managers at the hospital and that he was looking for a new head of development. I contacted him, offered him my services and we initiated a dialogue. I ended up getting the job.

In hindsight, it is interesting to reflect. upon the reactions I encountered from the people I knew. Many people, both inside and outside the healthcare sector, wished me good luck. At the same time, most people predicted that it would be difficult or more or less impossible. In other words, there was a perception that engaging in change efforts in the healthcare sector was difficult. A perception that has turned out not to be particularly accurate.

But it was clear that without an education and experience in the field of healthcare, I would face an uphill battle in my job developing the organization. This is not all that strange—this applies regardless of which sector you start working in! In such a case, it is not sufficient to enjoy the full confidence of the hospital director, the person who hired me. If you are to achieve something tangible, you need to create trust in the organization. Experiences from industries working with cellular systems, containers and ships don't always impress those working with life and death.

I was lucky! The head physician at SÄS at the time was well read in the field of lean management. The first time we met, he asked me which of all the books on lean I thought was the best. This was a difficult question as I hadn't read all that many. I had mostly learned through others and by experimenting myself. But we quickly bonded—he had broad theoretical knowledge and I was the self-taught practitioner. This alliance became extremely important, as we both learned a lot from each other and as we together could influence the development efforts at the hospital.

I have gradually formed more alliances, both internally and externally. Healthcare is an exciting sector since it is extremely transparent. The activities basically look more or less the same at all hospitals. A broken leg in Minneapolis should be looked after the same way as a broken leg in Miami. In addition, in most countries it is basically a tax-funded activity without any direct competition. This means that there is a weak basis for being secretive. Consequently, there is a significant willingness to learn and share experiences. We have engaged in a great deal of benchmarking.

Gone on and received many study visits and carried out research exchange programs in both Sweden and abroad.

When I arrived at SÄS, Peter Kammensjö [a lean consultant] had completed the lion's share of a lean course for the managers. The last session was about Hoshin Kanri, and it came naturally for Peter and me to share this session. After that, a number of slots for next year's strategy work had been booked. In hindsight, a crucial point in the change efforts was when we decided to throw out the old way of engaging in strategic planning and instead apply what we had discussed at the end of the course (i.e., Hoshin Kanri). No one at this time really knew how to do this in practice, but we had the courage to try. In hindsight it was a bold decision!

When we gathered at the first strategy meeting, SÄS had 12 key focus areas, 25–35 different strategies and programs (depending on how you counted) and 142 KPIs to report. There were seven governing bodies to which the hospital reported. At the first meeting, this excessive structure was completely cut to pieces when we tried to create a sense of focus in the organization. We concluded with five focus areas, 13 selected KPIs and 12 change programs. When we presented this to the wider group of managers, we expected a great deal of questioning and hesitation. To our surprise, however, the new proposal was unanimously accepted. It turned out that no one had any overview prior to this. But don't get me wrong. We still report 142 KPIs to seven governing bodies. The difference is that we don't try to *control* the organization by means of these KPIs. They rather serve as "reporting indicators." The KPIs we now use are even fewer than the 13 we arrived at in 2012.

We have now created a structure that is both understandable and logical, while at the same time reducing administrative work. This creates trust. When I talk about change efforts, I tend to use the analogy of managing capital in mutual funds. In change efforts, trust is our capital. It is a matter of placing as much trust as possible into the account—this may be necessary when you venture into something riskier. So, at first you have to carefully choose change projects and be almost certain that they will succeed. After ten such projects, you have accumulated enough capital to perhaps venture into something a little bit more risky.

A few years later, I now see that the change efforts were carried out much faster and more smoothly at SÄS than many assumed when they congratulated me on the new job. After six months, a full-scale Hoshin Kanri structure was in place at all clinics. But the change efforts don't end there. We have implemented more than a hundred improvements to the Hoshin Kanri process since 2012, and there is still much to be done. Because even though the level of openness to change has been greater than many people initially believed, many working methods and cultures take time to change.

Peter's story highlights four key success factors when engaging in change efforts. Do you give an affirmative answer to these four questions?

- Do you have the engagement and knowledge required to be a successful change agent?
- Are you lucky?
- Can you build momentum for change by using leverage effects?
- Can you identify "low-hanging fruits" leading to further changes?

In the introduction to Chapter 3, we asked if you, our reader, have the necessary engagement to work with Hoshin Kanri as well as what constitutes your drivers. In the case of Peter, he clearly possessed the necessary engagement. He truly glowed when talking about his work. He was engaged and he was self-confident. Self-confidence is related to knowledge. And even if Peter had no knowledge of the healthcare sector he was experienced in lean and Hoshin Kanri. If you don't own such experience or knowledge, you have a challenge. Here is one way to deal with this challenge. First, educate yourself! Attend a course, locate a mentor and/or study one more book after you read this! Then seek allies with whom you can initiate a learning journey together. Start with minor challenges, go under the radar and experiment together. The advantage is obvious; if successful you end up with a team of change agents that share the same experience, knowledge and engagement. A team you can work with when transforming your organization.

"Luck" is perhaps not the right word, even though what a famous athlete once said about luck provides food for thought: the more he practiced, the luckier he seemed to be. Let us call it positive coincidences. Coincidences worked in Peter's favor. SÄS had embarked on a lean journey. The hospital director knew where he wanted to go. The basic culture in the healthcare sector is also positive. It is evidence-based, meaning that the systematic scientific approach is familiar to decision-makers. When the time had come to introduce and implement, Peter's expertise was spot on.

The previous comment on luck may also be linked to the fact that it is a question of practicing one's ability to see opportunities and create leverage. If a meeting with decision-makers is booked for one purpose, is it possible to also use that meeting for another purpose? Can you create leverage by combining seemingly different projects occurring simultaneously? Can you link internal needs for change to important changes in the external environment, thus creating legitimacy? Some people seem to possess an innate talent to create these kinds of links. But there is nothing preventing the rest of us from practicing this.

The "low-hanging fruit" in the case of SÄS was the challenge of the complex reporting structure and all the KPIs. Simplifying and clarifying the hospital's mission was seen as positive, because no one likes unnecessary administration. Everyone wants to know which direction the organization is aiming for and feel that they are contributing to building something larger than themselves. The changes at SÄS made this clearer. To use Peter's words, a significant capital of trust was added to the account, and this capital served as the basis for future projects.

If we move on to a more general level, much of what we have discussed so far is about *power*. In some cultures you tend to avoid this topic, even though we all know that power is crucial for all forms of change efforts. The bad news is that unless you have power, you are not able to achieve all that much. The good news is that power is not static.

Power is affected by context. If you are employed as a cleaner at a Walmart department store, you don't have all that much power if you want to alter their strategy work. You are just one of about 2.1 million employees in the world's currently largest company (Wikipedia, 2021). But if you define your context as the cleaning department of your particular Walmart shop in Pahrump, Nevada (to use an example), you drastically increase the likelihood of you having the power to bring about change. The point of all this is that before you initiate change efforts, you should assess the potential for success. Assess the current conditions. What are the chances of success? Choose carefully!

Power also changes over time. By starting small, as we discussed and illustrated in Figure 4.1, you can gradually accumulate trust capital. Nor do you have to be a charismatic leader standing on the barricades. No, according to the leadership style advocated in Hoshin Kanri, transformational leadership, you should primarily work through others. It is by means of well-considered efforts to gain acceptance that you may achieve consensus regarding change—what is referred to as Nemawashi in Hoshin Kanri terms. (We discuss Nemawashi in more detail in Section 5.6.)

Finally, the need for power changes. If the culture in the organization is already in line with the seven principles of Hoshin Kanri, less change and trust are required to introduce this approach. If, on the other hand, there is an entrenched leadership style far from the transformational style, a lot of conflict in the management team and a lack of ambition, well, then you need a great deal of power to introduce Hoshin Kanri.

In the example in Box 4.9, the head of marketing at a medium-sized company had come to realize that his style would not work when he became CEO. He thus made a drastic attempt to change his leadership style.

BOX 4.9 CHANGE IN LEADERSHIP STYLE

The new CEO—let's call him Johan—had gathered all office workers for a joint workshop. The idea was to introduce Hoshin Kanri and let the group discuss the company's development. Johan had early on stated that he would not attend the workshop, as he wanted to let the group freely discuss the future of the company and avoid the previous leadership style, where the CEO had decided most things in an authoritarian style. He had written a document with his analysis and thoughts regarding the future, which he thought would serve as a point of departure in the group discussions. He pointed out that nothing was decided—objectives and plans were open to the group to decide.

Just before the workshop was to begin, Johan realized that he should nevertheless attend in order to answer questions. He then made a compromise: he attended the workshop but only as a passive participant. He managed to refrain from speaking, except when he was asked direct questions. And there were many such questions. It turned out that a great deal was unclear, as the previous CEO had kept a large amount of information to himself.

Johan described the role of the former CEO as a "problem-solver": he had fixed most things in the company, from getting new business to operating machines when there were no operators. Johan had a goal with his change in leadership style: not to be a problem-solver but to be a "support function." During the workshop, primarily the head of production and a project developer took a step forward and adopted leadership roles. After the workshop, these two became key players in the continued work to introduce Hoshin Kanri.

BOX 4.10 WANT TO LEARN MORE?

In Section 4.2, we introduced the choice to either focus on a specific challenge (large or small) when implementing Hoshin Kanri or implement the entire annual planning cycle at once. In the following text, Wiebe Nijdam, director at the Lean Management Instituut, discusses this alternative further: https://planet-lean.com/a-guide-to-practical-hoshin. This text originates from *Planet Lean*, the official online magazine of the Lean Global Network. You will find a great deal of relevant knowledge on this website.

We would like to recommend two articles on change processes that may interest you. In the first one, John Kotter's classic text on how to transform your organization, the perspective is that of the leader. Kotter assumes that you have power and work as a CEO or the like. Based on this, he identifies eight steps that the process of change goes through. An article by Johnson et al. adopts a somewhat different approach. The perspective is still that of management, but what is in focus here is not a change project but instead how some organizations can change in a profitable way over time.

- Kotter, J. (1995), Leading change: Why transformation efforts fail. *Harvard Business Review*, *73*(2), p. 59–67.
- Johnson, G., Yip, G. S. & Hensmans, M. (2012), Achieving successful strategic transformation. *MIT Sloan Management Review*, *53*(3), p. 25–32.

In this chapter, we have repeatedly concluded that driving change management requires engagement. Julie Gebauer and Don Lowman further analyze the concept of engagement in their book *Closing the Engagement Gap*. They identify five actions: know them, grow them, inspire them, involve them and reward them. There is no need to complicate matters!

- Gebauer, J. & Lowman, D. (2008), *Closing the Engagement Gap—How Great Companies Unlock Employee Potential for Superior Results*. London: Portfolio.

As discussed in this chapter, engagement may be expressed in different ways. Frustration expressed in the form of cursing and hate is one. Jay Baer has written a good book on business and hate!

- Baer, J. (2016), *Hug Your Haters: How to Embrace Complaints and Keep Your Customers*. New York: Portfolio.

Notes

1. From Wikipedia: "Zlatan Ibrahimović, born 1981, is a Swedish professional footballer. Ibrahimović is widely regarded as one of the best strikers of his generation and one of the most decorated active footballers in the world, having won 31 trophies in his career. He has played in Sweden, Holland, Italy, Spain, England, the US and Italy again." https://www.aftonbladet.se/sportbladet/fotboll/a/a2aLGL/battre-poangsnitt-utan-zlatan-i-laget
2. Unfortunately, this book, *Snabbväxarnas hemligheter*, is not available in English. A book based on the same approach and focus on frustration in order to identify business opportunities is Jay Baer's *Hug Your Haters: How to Embrace Complaints and Keep Your Customers*. His point is that haters are not the problem. The problem is that you don't embrace them!

Chapter 5

Hoshin in Hoshin Kanri

In Chapter 2, we described the visionary target condition when an organization is entirely engaged in working with Hoshin Kanri. This target condition was characterized by people working according to seven principles:

- Long-term thinking
- Change curiosity
- Focus
- Process orientation
- Visualization
- Managing by learning
- Facts that drive and decide

In Chapter 3, we analyzed the current condition of you and your organization, thus also the conditions for developing a Hoshin Kanri–inspired approach to strategy work. In Chapter 4, we introduced a few different ways of initiating the change efforts based on challenges; that is, by starting with a distinct challenge and thereby teaching the organization how to apply the Hoshin Kanri principles. This is followed by a systematic upscaling, in which you address increasingly greater challenges. The process is then concluded by introducing the entire annual planning cycle (see Figure 5.1).

In this chapter, we adopt more of a holistic approach to Hoshin Kanri. This means that we now assume that Hoshin Kanri is introduced in its entirety (i.e., the annual planning cycle) and then go into more detail on how an organization working with Hoshin Kanri designs its processes, methods and behaviors. This is the model said to have been introduced by Toyota.

DOI: 10.4324/9781003194811-5

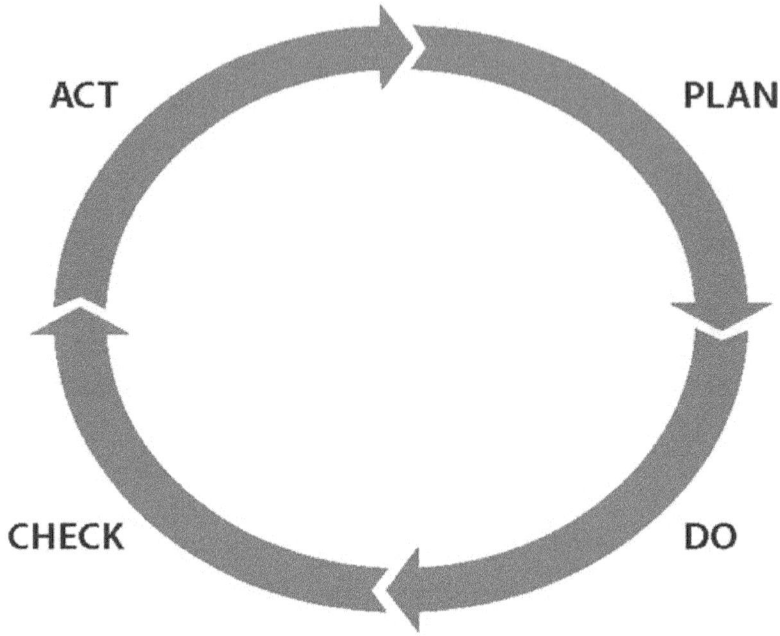

Figure 5.1 The Annual Planning Cycle

We have also come across other year-based models inspired by Hoshin Kanri but that don't really follow Toyota's approach. At the end of Chapter 6, we discuss these models in more depth.

5.1 Organizing the Introduction

Going all in from the outset and introducing year-based planning in its entirety is the approach described in all books we have read on Hoshin Kanri. The problem, however, is that Hoshin Kanri is not a regular change project. The decisive factor in Hoshin Kanri is that *top management* adopts the approach. When it comes to many other projects, these are OK'd by top management, after which the implementation is delegated to a project manager. This approach does not work when it comes to Hoshin Kanri.

As repeated on a number of occasions in the Lindbäcks case (see Appendix 1), a full-scale introduction of Hoshin Kanri is entirely dependent on top management making a clear commitment. Unless top management show engagement and makes a clear (and long-term) commitment, the introduction will eventually fail.

How, then, to create this commitment in top management? This is a tricky task since it is difficult to promise to be fully engaged in relation to something if you don't really know what the task entails. And when it comes to Hoshin Kanri, it is often the case that top management don't have experience and don't understand the pros and cons of this way of working. In this case, it is important to visualize a possible target condition. How to do that? Well, the simple answer, which we have already mentioned in Chapter 4, is learning trips. A learning trip is carefully planned. What do you want to study? Why should you study this? How are you to document and evaluate the knowledge obtained? And how is it to be used? A trip also enables you to discuss different issues internally within the group. What do you want to achieve during the trip with regard to internal change? Think Nemawashi! (We return to this in Section 5.6.) If you ask these types of questions, the visit will be a learning trip. You can go on leisure trips when you're not working.

Involving consultants is an interesting question. Compared to a learning trip for the entire management team, it is easier to invite a consultant to talk about these things. However, this is never as good as getting first-hand information and experiencing something for yourself. Don't get us wrong, consultants can play a major role in the introduction phase, but there is a risk that management will leave it up to the consultants to introduce the approach. If you choose the right consultant, things will probably work out fine at first, but what happens when the consultant leaves? Does management take the baton and set the direction? Or do the consultants take the approach with them as they walk through the door? At Lindbäcks, they eventually hired several of the consultants they contracted at the beginning of the introduction, which is a possible solution. In what we consider the best book on Hoshin Kanri, Cowley and Domb's *Beyond Strategic Vision* (1997), the authors highlight the importance of top management's commitment, arguing that it takes at least five days of full-time work for the management team to truly understand what Hoshin Kanri really entails. Not only does it involve learning the approach, but it also involves understanding whether it suits the organization. Five days in a four-member management team equals one month of work—a substantial investment just to evaluate whether to invest!

In the Lindbäcks case, the project manager repeatedly emphasized that they should have worked more with the management team during the initial stage. This is about getting the management team to make *a* commitment and, not least, that the management team makes the *same* commitment.

Once management has made a commitment, the next step is to create a *project team*. The composition and size of this team naturally depend on the size of the organization, but regardless of size, the head of the organization needs to be an active participant in the team. In smaller organizations, a common approach is that a project manager works closely with the CEO, while more people need to be involved in larger organizations. In several cases we have encountered, the role of project manager for Hoshin Kanri is combined with working as a lean coach or head of quality. Regardless of the exact structure, it is worth repeating that the CEO or owner needs to take the ultimate responsibility while also clearly demonstrating this. Don't forget the principle of long-term thinking. Those with power must show that this is a change they support and intend to pursue with a long-term perspective. Otherwise, the organization will be better off spending its investment funds in another area.

An introduction project takes time. A rule of thumb is to spend the first year getting the management team on board; in other words, the goal is to introduce Hoshin Kanri to the management team in year one, then in year two get the rest of the organization on board. In practice, this would mean that the goal in year one is to create a common understanding of both the objectives and the direction of the organization and how the strategy work should be designed in the management team. In year two, the annual negotiations in the Hoshin phase are then moved down in the organization ("catchballs"; see Section 5.5) and clearer methods for follow-up and learning are introduced.

After these two years, the role of project manager can be transformed into the role of *process owner*. Setting the standard and working with continuous development requires a designated process owner. However, the shift from project manager to process owner in no way implies that the introduction has been completed. Almost two decades have passed since Toyota took over BT Industries in Sweden and Toyota Material Handling Europe was formed. As to whether BT has now fully implemented Hoshin Kanri, the answer is definitely no. There is always potential for improvement when working in a Toyota company. Processes are never optimal. Everyone we have encountered gives the same answer. At Lindbäcks, they say that it is too early to talk about a standard—they have only used the annual planning cycle for four years and make significant improvements each time.

The background, experience and personality of the project manager or process owner play a key role in the Hoshin Kanri process. For example, the first step in the process is to determine the vision of the organization. This work is aimed at the owners of the organization and often requires a certain amount of authority to moderate. But things don't end there. There is a constant need for "rules police" in the organization, someone who embodies the Hoshin Kanri principles and is not afraid to question management's behaviors. No wonder many of the process owners we have encountered have a long and broad experience, frequently as a result of having held several management positions in the organization.

A good process owner focuses on the whole picture (i.e., beyond the process at hand). With regard to the Hoshin Kanri process, this means that the process owner must also spend time identifying processes with an impact on the strategy process and determine how these processes relate to each other. In many organizations, the budget process is crucial. The question here is whether and how it should be linked to the strategy work. Another process to consider is the human resource development process. For example, performance reviews can be linked to activities in the strategy work.

The process owner is also responsible for the toolbox, meaning the set of analytical tools planned to be used in the strategy work (and hopefully in other contexts as well). In Chapter 7, we describe some of the most commonly used tools in organizations working with Hoshin Kanri.

BOX 5.1 UNANIMOUS MANAGEMENT TEAM

Many years ago, one of us attended a media and communications course. This course was organized by a well-known communications agency. At the first session, the experienced consultant shared a story that took place during the financial crisis in the early 1990s. The consultant had been contracted by a bank to train the management team on how to communicate with the media.

To get a good start in the course, the consultant decided to stop the management team members when they arrived at the headquarters in the morning. They were taken one by one to a room where they were subjected to a rapid-fire interview on current issues. Once the consultant had interviewed everyone, he met the entire management team and played back the interviews. The effect of this exercise was that the communications training was canceled. It turned out that the CEO was very upset when she heard the responses given by the various team members. These short interviews clearly showed that the management team was not unanimous. They gave completely different answers to the same questions. How was the team to lead the bank in the same direction when they couldn't even agree on which direction to go?

5.2 Developing and Gaining Acceptance for the Target Condition

With regard to the entire fiscal year, the concepts of planning, execution and follow-up can be linked to the concepts of Hoshin and Kanri. Hoshin refers to the process of how to identify and gain acceptance for the *target condition*. Kanri, on the other hand, focuses on the *execution* of all activities and the *follow-up* and learning.

The division into Hoshin (planning phase) and Kanri (management and follow-up phase) can easily be seen as the same division between formulating and implementing found in traditional strategy work. That is a mistake. In Hoshin Kanri, a large part of the organization is involved in the Hoshin phase, defining its own objectives and action plans (i.e., what we refer to as *activities* from now on). In traditional strategy work, typically a few individuals (e.g., the management team) develop the plan to subsequently be implemented throughout the organization.

In Hoshin Kanri, implementation, follow-up and possible modification (Kanri) represent crucial elements, and this is done in a systematized way. The focus on this phase offers room for corrections and changes, in addition to an opportunity to evaluate and learn. This is given less space in traditional strategy work. A difference is also that learning does not primarily focus on the outcome, but on the process. In traditional strategic work, management may adjust the plan if the desired outcome does not materialize or if there are changes in the external environment. However, this occurs with a significant amount of delay, as it takes time for the signals to reach management. In Hoshin Kanri, you may, if necessary, adjust activity plans at several different levels in the organization at regular follow-up meetings, even if this is done very reluctantly. The most important aspect, however, concerns the efforts related to developing and refining the process. Based on the principle of focusing on the process, there is an assumption that a well-functioning process generates good results. "Well-functioning" here refers to a process having been repeated several times and continuously developed and improved.

Hoshin in Kanri consists of different layers (Figure 5.2). The annual planning cycle contains several shorter cycles. At the same time, the one-year planning cycle we choose to focus on in this book is not the outermost layer; rather, this cycle should be linked to the organization's visionary target condition, which may be five to ten years into the future.

Long-term thinking was the first principle for Hoshin Kanri we identified in Chapter 2. There, we defined it as

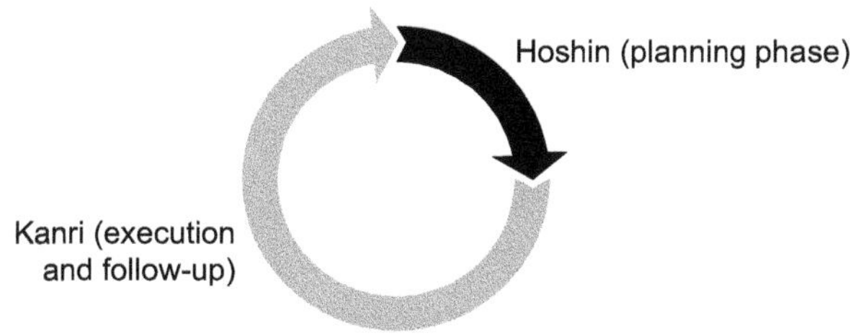

Figure 5.2 Planning, Execution and Follow-Up

a desire to systematically develop the organization toward a clearly formulated and communicated vision intending to create long-term value for the organization and its stakeholders, [which] is a fundamental prerequisite for being successful when adopting Hoshin Kanri.

BOX 5.2 GREAT COMPANIES

The book *Good to Great* was published in 2004, and it summarized a very ambitious study on great companies. In this study, Jim Collins made an important decision. He adopted a more long-term perspective than most popular management books and studied companies that performed very well for 15 years. The reason for this decision was that many companies receiving a great deal of attention have a charismatic CEO for a period of seven or eight years. The success of these companies is often clearly linked to the specific period of having this CEO. When the CEO leaves the company, the company's performance goes down. In a great company, more permanent structures are created (however, nothing lasts forever). Some of the interesting results in Collins' book include that the leadership of these companies was characterized by exceptional personal humility and professional desire. The leaders were people who drove the organization forward but never focused on their own wealth and career. They were happy to hire highly qualified employees, more qualified than they were. They paid employees well and trusted that they were independent (within certain limits). They created a culture characterized by focus and discipline and where facts rule. Bitter truths were welcome! As we can see, this long-term leadership style corresponds well with the principles characterizing Hoshin Kanri.

There are three reasons for this conclusion. First, a clearly formulated and communicated vision means that the members of the organization have been given the ability to work in the right direction. Second, long-term thinking creates a sense of security, which, in turn, enables investing in long-term changes. These investments are not necessarily recouped in the short term. Companies such as Toyota and IKEA adopt a long-term perspective and consider themselves good citizens of society—they have formulated a purpose beyond making their owners rich. Third, and linked to this, long-term continuity is created by the fact that the organization's objectives are hopefully overruling the sometimes short-term interests of management.

5.3 The Task of the Owners: Deciding the Direction

In Chapter 2, we discussed visions and a visionary target condition. We now discuss this line of reasoning in somewhat more depth. We could have chosen to use "deciding the vision" in the heading, but it is unnecessary to focus on the word vision when what matters here is that the organization needs a *direction*, something that creates meaning for the employees in the sense that it is clear and inspiring. This direction does not have to be described in a formal vision document. Sometimes, it is described in the organization's corporate governance document. In other cases, the direction may be indicated in a values document, in long-term objectives or in the business idea. To once again paraphrase *Alice in Wonderland*, you need to know where you're going to know which direction to go. The owners or management of the organization thus need to determine a *target condition*, perhaps three to five years into the future—a condition that is challenging and engaging and that requires considerable efforts to achieve. Before proceeding, we would like to once again emphasize that we use the term owner in a broad sense as we refer to those who determine the mission of the organization (unit, department, section, etc.), meaning the individual or individuals expecting a combined result from the efforts undertaken by the organization and with the power to change the organization's conditions.

Let's apply the basic technique in Hoshin Kanri to the work on creating a vision. The first step in determining the target condition is to *analyze the current condition*. Is there currently anything written down indicating the direction of the organization? Is this something that is engaging and communicated in the organization? After analyzing the

BOX 5.3 VISIONARY?

So, how far into the future should you look to be visionary? Earlier, we wrote that the vision should extend three to five years into the future. This only applies to some extent, as time is relative. What is fast for one individual is slow for another. This applies both to exercising and to working. Some people are always on the go, while others like to take it easy. But this does not decide who is stressed or has a breakdown. We would argue that the same applies to organizations. Some departments are living life in the fast lane, while others have a slower pace. This typically also applies in terms of hierarchy: the owners put pressure on the CEO for things to happen quickly, which means that the CEO is often impatient and expects a higher pace than the rest of the organization does. There are also differences between different types of organizations. The pace in some digitalized industries is high, while it may be significantly slower in other industries. This is frequently linked to technical or structural factors.

Which time perspective is the most suitable for your organization? Is a vision spanning two years into the future reasonable? Or are you going to set a vision ten years from now? What is your pace?

current conditions, the vision should be formulated. Which values should characterize the vision? In this phase, it is important to take ownership into account (i.e., who owns the work to create a vision). Far too frequently, only a few, or perhaps just one person, create the vision. The result may be good, but it will never be really good unless the entire organization experiences a sense of ownership—that they have been involved in developing the vision, thereby also taking responsibility for the implementation.

One way of creating this form of ownership in the organization is for the owners to refrain from making the vision too detailed. The owners may choose to be either "precisely imprecise"—for example, by setting a long-term yield requirement (e.g., a 10 percent increase in operating profits within five years), or imprecise in general, by simply indicating a direction (e.g., striving for diversity in the housing market). In the next step, the owners may then entrust the management team with developing the organization's visionary target condition (i.e., describing how the organization operates when the vision has been achieved). If the management team and the owners can agree on the vision and the target condition developed based on this vision, both parties will feel that they own the vision, which leads to engagement in the continued process.

In Table 5.1, we have formulated four questions that may be helpful when creating a vision.

There are two major pitfalls that should be avoided at this stage. The first is getting bogged down in a discussion on the current condition. (What do things actually look like at this moment in time?) The second concerns the fact that it is easy to lose focus and get caught up in discussions on what the future should look like.

There are obviously good reasons for properly analyzing both issues. Not agreeing on the current condition makes predicting the future quite difficult. And trying to predict the future is always to some extent speculative, something that may go on forever. This means that a great deal of time and resources are spent on various studies.

It is also difficult to give clear advice on what the balance should look like between thorough analysis work and the time (and other resources) invested. However, one piece of advice is to listen to Voltaire, who said, "Perfect is the enemy of good." In other words, accept something that is not perfect in order to move forward in the process. If you do, you will frequently learn more than when you get bogged down in studies. If you move forward in the process, it is always possible to learn from it and develop it by next year. If you don't move forward, this is not possible. Note that we write, "get bogged down in studies." By this, we

Table 5.1 Guiding Questions for Developing a Vision

Today	*In the future*
Who is your customer? (You probably have many customers, but try to describe your ideal customer.)	Who will be your ideal customer?
Who is your competition in terms of the ones satisfying the needs of your ideal customer?	Who will be your competition in terms of the ones satisfying the needs of your ideal customer in the future?
Which skills and types of expertise form the basis of your competitiveness?	Which skills and types of expertise will form the basis of your competitiveness?
Why do your customers choose you?	Why will your customers choose you?

mean that it is important to have a good balance between analyzing and conducting a thorough discussion with many people in the organization before deciding on a vision. You should allocate time for this discussion. It is better to have general acceptance for the vision than a perfect formulation!

5.4 The Task of Management: Identifying the Organization's Challenges

When the vision is decided and has gained acceptance among the owners, the organization is the one to answer the question of how to achieve it. The first step in these efforts is to identify the major challenges. In Hoshin Kanri terms, this is often referred to as breakthroughs.

Major challenges may take many different forms. Sometimes, they only describe the area you need to address: processes, brand, leadership, and so on. In other cases, the challenge is more narrowly defined, such as "strengthening our market position in Eastern Europe," "developing our supply chain" or "developing future retirement homes in terms of digitalization." The aim should be to identify broad challenges rich in content. Limiting the major challenge to a single function—such as deciding that the challenge should be to develop our production—doesn't offer all that much guidance.

It is important to keep in mind that you should identify only a limited number of major challenges, perhaps just three or four. There are two reasons for this. The first is that a small number of challenges offers focus and direction. This means that you can actually achieve substantial change within a defined area since you prioritize and pool your resources. Remember the principle of focusing in Chapter 2.

The second reason is that if you have a small number of challenges, your organization must work across functions. In other words, organizational functions must work together not only to understand the challenge, but also to address it by means of effective activities.

In order to create learning between departments and functions and create a breeding ground for more innovative solutions, everyone needs to ask themselves how they can contribute in their own function to solving a challenge that does not primarily concern their own field of operations. In this situation, however, it is common that you end up in a somewhat political

BOX 5.4 FOCUSING

Here is how Mark DeLuzio, working at Lean Horizons Consulting and former CEO of Danaher, where he introduced Hoshin Kanri, has described the importance of focusing:

> The key is focus on the critical few. The hardest thing to do with Hoshin is not figuring out what you are going to do . . . it's agreeing on what you are *not* going to do. Hoshin planning is all about focus.

The problem of focusing on only a few challenges has been a big issue in the examples from both SÄS and Lindbäcks. We have encountered many other organizations that have experienced the same problem.

negotiation based on the notion that "everyone" (all functions, all members of the management team, etc.) must have their own challenge. This is the easiest approach, while also seemingly fair. However, management often ends up identifying a list of challenges based on how the organization is organized (e.g., a challenge for each function represented in the management team). This way, everyone gets something to work with and no one has to leave their own sandbox. A good recipe for failure . . .

Box 5.5 presents a fictional example of an organization having identified challenges that may be very relevant individually. When combined, however, the result is not good.

BOX 5.5 FUNCTION-BASED BEHAVIOR

At the last management team meeting, the company Function, Ltd., decided that these five challenges were to be addressed in the following year:

- HR—Our challenge is to create an attractive workplace for millennials.
- Production—Our challenge is to create stable flows.
- Finance—Our challenge is to create processes capable of managing volatility in exchange rates.

- Marketing—Our challenge is to increase customer satisfaction in order to retain existing customers.
- Purchasing—Our challenge is to reduce the share of material costs in existing products.

When the top managers in Function, Ltd., left the meeting and went back to start working with their employees on the agreed-upon challenges, the focus was on solving "their" challenge. There was no cooperation across boundaries, and activities and measurable objectives ended up in conflict with each other later in the process. If, instead, the management team of Function, Ltd., had decided to focus on one or two challenges over the coming year, the organizational structures would also have been challenged. What if the marketing department's customer satisfaction challenge had been selected? What can the finance department do to retain customers? How can production contribute? And how can purchasing make a contribution? These issues are challenging and can result in innovative ideas. By wrestling with them, you also learn of the other functions in your organization. If you focus like this, a function may not be directly affected by the selected challenges. Apart from helping other functions solve the organization's chosen challenges, they may have a little less Hoshin Kanri work to do that year and can work more on continuous improvement. Next year will be different.

Perhaps you noticed that a few of the challenges in Figure 5.3 are not directly in the path toward the vision. They are there to remind us that it is important to analyze which challenges truly matter. Quite often, a number of challenges are always mentioned when discussing the future. Perhaps it is time to question these. Do these really constitute the most important major challenges?

In Chapter 7, we describe the A3 tool in more detail, but here we want to show how working on creating a vision may be described in an A3 format.

As shown in Figure 5.4, you start with analyzing the current condition, followed by identifying the target condition (in this case the vision) and then, finally, analyzing the gap between the two. At this overall level, this leads to you identifying three or four major challenges for the organization. The challenge will be to solve these challenges within the defined time period.

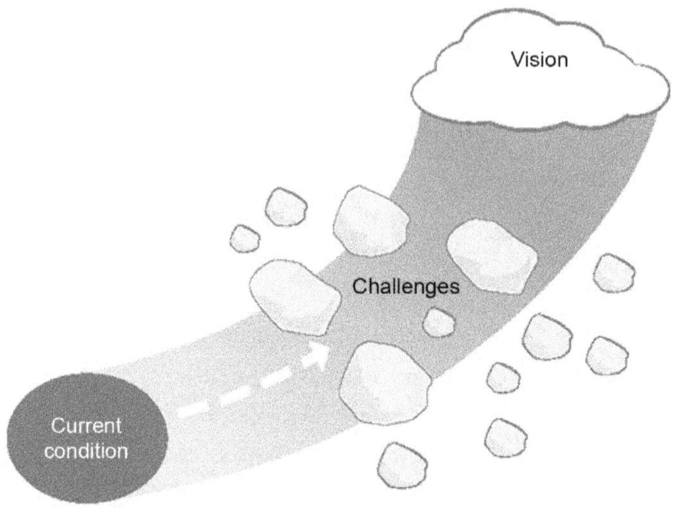

Figure 5.3 Focus on Challenges

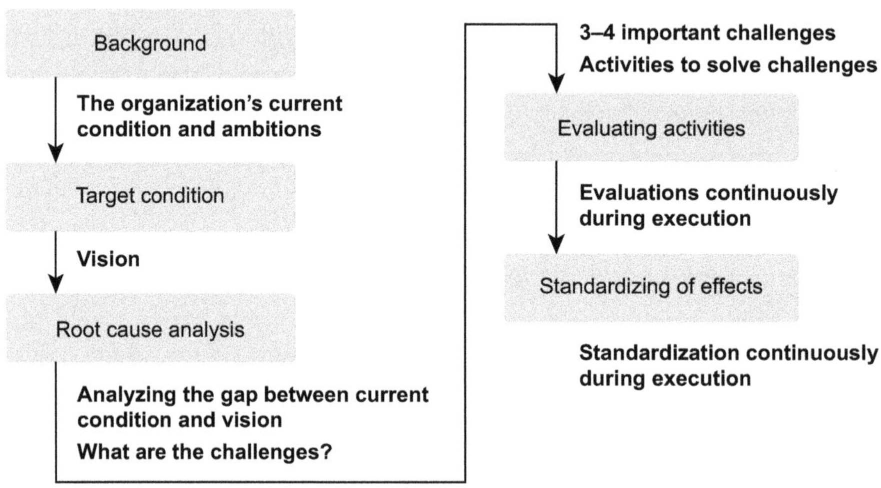

Figure 5.4 Visionary A3

BOX 5.6 DOES THE CHALLENGE MATTER?

In a course we offered, there were participants from a public organization. When we started talking about vision, one of them immediately brought up recruitment as their greatest challenge. He had good reasons for this. The organization was not ranked among the top ten most popular employers and it was not located in the hottest labor market region.

Regardless, was it obvious that their largest challenge was recruitment. This issue was discussed back and forth, after which an important decision was made: to put the matter on hold for a while. The reason was that it was not possible to decide whether recruitment was the main challenge, simply because the organization's vision had not yet been determined. Once again, if you don't know in which direction you are going, it is impossible to know which challenge is most the most important.

5.5 From Major Challenges to This Year's Planning: "Catchball"

We now go from the long-term visionary target condition and the major challenges to the one-year planning cycle.

According to the Hoshin Kanri terminology, we have now entered the "catchball" phase. This is when the organization negotiates what it will achieve during the coming year. The term catchball means that this negotiation should include several iterations: the ball—or in this case, perceptions and ambitions—is thrown back and forth. The result of this process should be an organizational set of objectives and activities clearly linked to the people responsible and having defined powers. These objectives and activities should be clearly linked to quantified measures. These measures are not always easy to identify, but without clarity in terms of reaching the objectives, it will be difficult to evaluate and learn from the activities.

If you choose to organize the strategy work in accordance with the organization's organizational structure (as we have assumed so far), it is crucial that you have reached a consensus regarding the vision and challenges at the management level before you proceed. If there is no consensus on the overall direction, there is no point in continuing to introduce Hoshin Kanri. In such a case, the employees will simply run in different directions. A lack of clarity regarding the objective (vision) and major challenges at the management level undoubtedly creates major problems further down in the organization.

The fact that management agrees on the vision or direction does not necessarily mean that they agree on what is to be achieved during the coming year. In fact, easily coming to an agreement on what is to be achieved in the near future actually indicates a problem. This indicates that the objective is not sufficiently ambitious and that it is time to raise the level of ambition.

The whole process from target condition to action may thus be described as a friendly (but sometimes tough) negotiation—a negotiation in which all participants agree on the long-term target condition and now together explore how to jointly achieve this condition. If the one-year objective is sufficiently challenging, there must be some give and take at all levels in order to agree on the best way to achieve the objective.

The CEO frequently makes the first move in the negotiation. Here, the CEO informs the functional managers in the management team of what must be done if the vision is to be achieved within the specified timeframe. For example, the objective for year one could be to solve one of the three or four major challenges identified.

The questions all functional managers now need to ask themselves are more general in nature: Is what the CEO thinks should be done the most effective way of achieving the vision? Is it possible to achieve what the CEO wants to do during the year? To answer these questions, each functional manager in the management team, together with their employees, must begin by analyzing the CEO's position. Do we understand what the CEO really wants? And, not least: Has the CEO made a correct analysis and formulated the best short-term objective, given the target condition?

Note that in this first phase, it is not a question of discussing the level of ambition, but the focus is on the objective itself. Is it the right type of annual objective to achieve over time the long-term target condition of the organization? Consensus on these issues needs to be achieved before you can discuss the level of ambition in phase two. This is an important point. If the level of ambition and the relevance of the objective are intertwined in the negotiation, this often leads to confusion and conflicts. So, make sure you all agree on what you negotiate about before you enter the negotiation!

After the initial analysis, which may result in the CEO and the management team having to engage in an initial negotiation on the direction for the coming year, the time has come for phase two: analyzing the conditions for achieving the objective. What does the current condition look like in my department or function? Which changes in our external environment may we anticipate in our function? And, given this analysis, what is required of us in our function or department to achieve the proposed one-year objective? For example, does reaching this objective require us to collaborate with other functions? If the answer to the last question is yes, these functions must obviously be contacted and engaged in separate negotiations.

BOX 5.7 NEGOTIATION AND CONSENSUS

In this book, we frequently use the terms negotiation and consensus. We look upon negotiation as something positive. It is about jointly agreeing on what the current condition looks like as well as an objective or target condition that is possible to achieve. This means that the meaning of this type of negotiation is not that someone should win. On the contrary, this negotiation process should lead to something better than the original standpoints—something better that we all agree on. Sometimes, it is not possible to achieve complete consensus, but it is important to ensure that everyone involved understands and accepts the decision that is finally made. If you achieve this, you have achieved a great deal.

In Box 5.8, we have summarized the aforementioned negotiation in four key questions that the functional managers (and all other subsequent employees) should reflect upon when they have received the objective. These questions must be answered before the next stage of the negotiation begins.

BOX 5.8 FOUR KEY QUESTIONS

For functional managers (and for everyone else in subsequent negotiations):

- What do the owners/CEO really expect?
- What is the view of our function in terms of what is possible to achieve?
- What happens in our environment that is specifically affecting us in our function (both the environment inside our organization and the broader external environment)?
- Which lessons from our operations (our function) affect our assessment of what is possible to achieve?

In a well-functioning Hoshin process, this is just the beginning of several iterations between the CEO and other members of the management team. These iterations (or steps in the negotiation) are both horizontal and vertical. The functional manager must negotiate horizontally to understand both the current conditions thoroughly and make agreements with other stakeholders on what is achievable. Then the functional manager must negotiate the objective with the CEO. Perhaps, as a result of this, the CEO must adjust the original one-year objective.

Figure 5.5 specifies the objective of the first year as eliminating a major challenge on the path toward the vision.

Earlier, we described the decision regarding the one-year objective as a negotiation between the CEO and functional managers in the management team. However, such a negotiation should involve many more individuals. The CEO may appoint a "negotiation team" to which they may delegate the negotiation. In turn, functional managers may include many individuals within their respective functions in order to determine what is possible to achieve. In principle, the more people are involved in this phase, the better. If more people are involved, the "counteroffer" of the functional managers to the CEO will be more credible and enjoy more acceptance. It would be a pity if, after long negotiations with the CEO, the functional managers were to arrive at a one-year objective that they then fail to gain acceptance for in their respective functions.

Now that we have taken an additional step in the Hoshin process, we may describe it in a new A3. The overall steps—the vision and the three to four challenges—have now turned into inputs in the process of describing the background and identifying the current condition. A one-year objective was then decided upon. The "gap analysis" has identified challenges for achieving the one-year objective, which has then resulted in a number of activities (or Hoshin points) for this year (i.e., descriptions of various activities; see Figure 5.6).

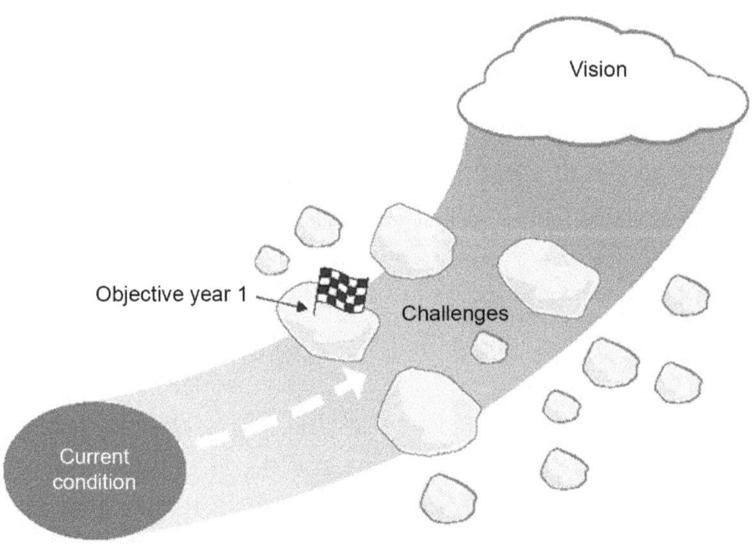

Figure 5.5 Visionary A3

BOX 5.9 CHALLENGING CHALLENGE?

On one of our study visits, we visited Mats Karlström, a lean manager at Saab Aerostructures. At Aerostructures, they had worked based on the Hoshin Kanri principles for more than five years. We learned a great deal during this visit. One of the most important lessons concerned the Hoshin process at the management level. Mats summed up his experiences with regard to this:

- *Purpose*: A dialogue in the organization regarding strategies, objectives and activity plans. Make sure we work on things we need to do, not just things we can do which are two completely different things.
- *Objectives*: Management understands that the strategies are achievable, which means that we will achieve our objectives. The organization understands our strategies and is actively involved in the question of how we implement strategies and achieve our objectives. Managers/leaders at all levels make commitments by deciding what we should do to achieve the objectives. The result is broad acceptance in terms of what needs to be done, which efforts will be required and what this will cost.
- *How*: Clarify the challenges. Many iterations are made within the management team and among the managers at the large departments. Management decides how possible remaining gaps should be addressed to achieve the objectives.

With regard to the question as to what represented their greatest challenge in this area, Mats replied that they were *too much in agreement* in the management team. There was nothing left that the CEO had to make a final decision on after the negotiations! He looked upon this as an indication that the challenges and objectives were too comfortable. The challenges must initially come across as truly challenging for there to be a good negotiation, where new solutions are jointly created. Otherwise, this is all for show. Note that by using the term negotiation, Mats implied jointly developing new solutions to the challenge. This did not refer to a negotiation in the sense of a tug-of-war within the framework of an existing solution. (See also the prior discussion on consensus.)

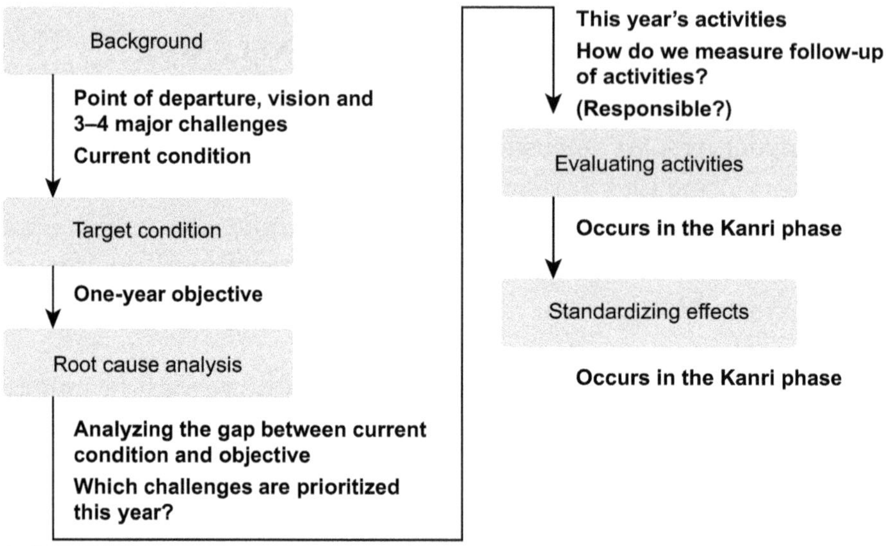

Figure 5.6 A3 for the Annual Planning Cycle

The chain continues accordingly. Earlier, we discussed only three levels with the positions of owner, CEO and functional managers. In the next stage, the functional managers, together with their respective functions, create a new A3 based on the inputs obtained in the previous negotiations. Basically, all employees in the organization could have their own A3. Typically, however, you stop at some level down in the organization, such as the departmental level. This ends the process by creating an A3 for the department, which designates people at the department responsible for different activities. This A3 may then be described as the department's summary of activities for that year.

In Figure 5.7, we have graphically described a possible outcome of the Hoshin phase during a one-year period. The organization's one-year target condition and four activities or challenges have been identified. Functions Y and Z have one activity each, one of which also overlaps with function X, which also has two other additional activities. Based on this, function X has identified three activities addressing one of their challenges as well as a fourth activity addressing both of the function's challenges. At the next level, there are a number of departments within function X having formulated activities linked to the overall activities of the function. Finally, the individuals in the team have some individual activities linked to one of the team's challenges.

Assuming that each individual has four activities and that the organization has 100 employees, there will be a total of 400 activities in one year. It

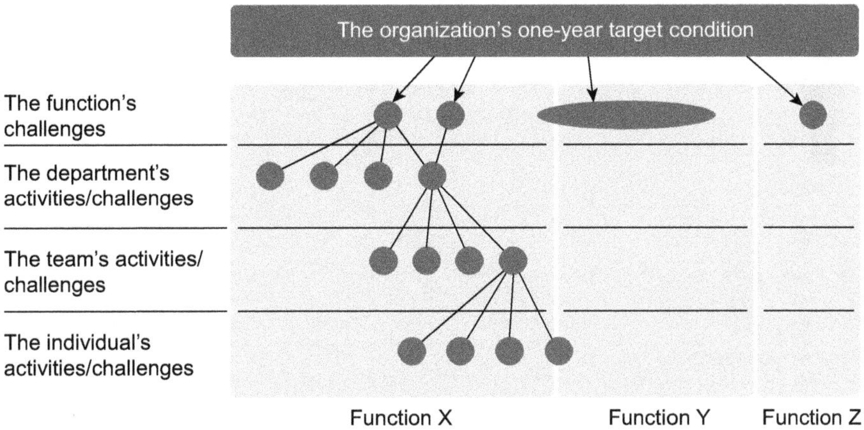

Figure 5.7 A3 Possible Hoshin Structure in an Organization

is possible to make two reflections in relation to this. First, an overview of the activities needs to be created relatively quickly in order to enable follow-up and avoid duplication of work. Second, and perhaps most important, there needs to be focus or else the work will be all over the place. One idea is to stop at the team level and avoid individual-based activities. If the 100 employees are divided into ten teams with five activities each, the subsequent total of 50 activities represents a much more manageable number.

Yet another reason for choosing carefully and choosing fewer activities is that this enables picking activities that cross boundaries and require cooperation.

If we return to the Hoshin process, the first goal is thus to reach consensus in the organization's management team regarding the one-year target condition. One consequence of these efforts to reach consensus is that activities seeking to achieve the objective begin to be clarified. This constitutes an obvious "side effect" when functional managers and their employees evaluate the possibility of achieving the proposed target condition. In other words, the organization has now started to formulate a hypothesis on what needs to be done to achieve the agreed-upon target condition. This hypothesis is then tested in the execution phase.

Previously, we wrote that the initial negotiations between the CEO and the functional managers in the management team might be extended to involve more people within the respective function. Depending on how many have been involved in this part of the process, the next step in the catchball efforts will differ in scope. However, the principle is the same. The objectives, having achieved consensus at one level, serve as the starting offers for negotiations with the next level. In an ultimate situation, these negotiations occur

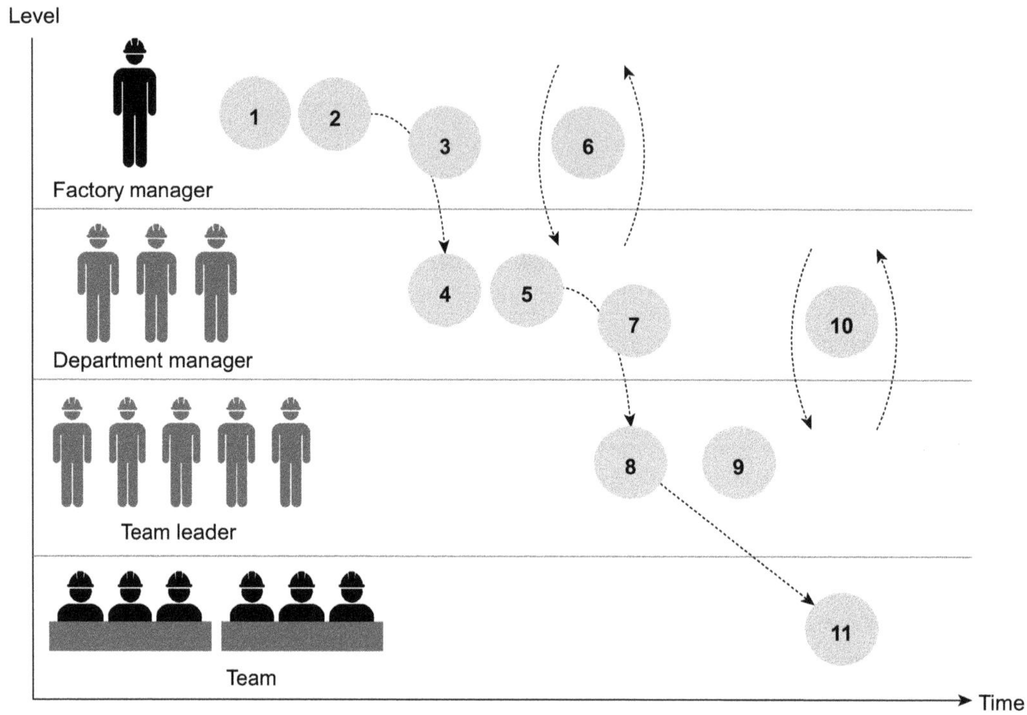

1. The factory's challenge(s) and objective(s) for the year is determined after the factory manager has negotiated with company management.
2. The factory manager details current conditions and describes the target condition.
3. The factory manager presents the current condition and target condition to department managers.
4. The department managers detail current conditions and describe target condition to their respective departments.
5. The department managers identify dependencies between processes and departments.
6. The department managers present the detailed current condition and target condition to the factory manager. Do these detailed descriptions match the factory manager's target condition?
7. The department managers present the current condition and target condition to team leaders.
8. The team leaders detail the current condition and describe the target condition to their respective teams.
9. The team leaders identify dependencies between teams (in a department).
10. The team leaders present detailed current conditions and target condition to the department manager. Do these detailed conditions match the department manager's target condition?
11. The team leaders present the current condition and target condition to their employees. Execution (Kanri) can begin.

Figure 5.8 Catchball at a Factory

throughout the organization. In most cases, however, you tend to stop at the frontline managers. In Figure 5.8, we describe four different levels.

5.6 Nemawashi

Nemawashi is a key concept in Hoshin Kanri. We mentioned it briefly in the previous chapter, but the time has now come to discuss it a bit further.

Nemawashi is about informal negotiations, meaning informal contacts between people where different ideas are tested and solutions gain acceptance.

Nemawashi is closely linked to the Hoshin Kanri principle of managing by learning, which we introduced in Chapter 2. We argued that one of the most important tasks for the leader is to develop and challenge the employees so that both the leader and the employees learn more. This coaching leadership is key for Nemawashi.

In an organization characterized by Hoshin Kanri, Nemawashi will inevitably play a major role. Not just because the ongoing "pre-negotiations" enable the people involved to revise and develop their positions—without a risk of losing face, but also because the existence of Nemawashi also means that strategy work is alive in day-to-day work. Strategy is discussed not only at a few individual meetings; instead, strategic questions are naturally tied into the day-to-day contacts in the organization.

In an organization characterized by Nemawashi, it is also easy to see the benefits of the A3 philosophy. In such an organization, the functional manager can bring their A3 sheet when informally discussing their positions with other employees. They can base their discussion on the A3 and agree to revise it. The A3 thus acts as a living protocol that is easy to carry while offering an overview of the situation. At the formal meeting, the functional manager can then take out their A3, describing the outcome of all informal negotiations, and obtain a formal stamp of approval. At least, this is what occurs in the best of worlds.

BOX 5.10 INVOLVE MORE!

A participant in one of our courses was very engaged and knowledgeable. He embarked on the Hoshin Kanri efforts with great enthusiasm, at the next meeting presenting a thorough analysis, challenges and activities in the form of an A3. After discussing the content for a while, however, we realized that all this work had occurred in his office behind closed doors. No one else in the organization had any knowledge of this work. There was no consensus on the problem formulation, analysis or conclusions in his organization. When he realized this, he went back to his organization and reworked it, this time together with his employees.

In other words, this person realized the problem and started all over from the beginning. The work now took much longer and he encountered a lot of problems. But by walking around and talking to the people concerned, two things happened. First, new facts came to light that improved the analysis. And perhaps more important, people became aware of the challenge and engaged in solving it. And once the new version of the A3 had been created, it was easy to get the activities started. Now everyone involved was ready to go.

Nemawashi is a concept linked to culture. Saito (1982) defines Nemawashi as the "Japanese form of interpersonal communication." Here, we don't discuss the Japanese culture in depth, nor do we compare it with other national cultures (if you are interested, see "Want to learn more?" at the end of this chapter). However, it is interesting to reflect upon what the culture in your own organization looks like and how it affects the decision-making processes.

When we wrote this section in the book, we started to discuss how Nemawashi materializes in various organizations. Based on this creative discussion, we created a small table (see Table 5.2) based on the dimensions *informal discussion and gaining acceptance* and *type of meetings.* You may look upon this table as inspiration for your own analysis. Perhaps this categorization will serve as a complement to your own Readiness Analysis.

5.7 When, Where and How?

If we assume that the fiscal year follows the calendar year, the Hoshin phase in Hoshin Kanri will take place in the fall. When and how long it lasts depends on how many people and iterations are involved. The first phase of the Hoshin efforts may be completed in a few days; for instance, by the management team going away on a planning meeting during which the negotiations on objectives for the next year are carried out in intense iterations. This is not advisable, since there is a great risk that the results of such planning meetings will only gain acceptance in the management team. At the other extreme, these efforts may take several months, as employees at different levels are invited to provide input and identify the activities they will be working on during the next year before the organization's final one-year target condition is established.

Table 5.2 Nemawashi—Six Types of Informal Negotiation

	Long, formal meetings in which matters are analyzed and decided	*Formal meetings to confirm what has already been decided*	*No formal meetings*
No informal discussion or gaining of acceptance	Organization characterized by formalized decision-making processes (e.g., organizations spread out geographically and temporally and/or public organizations)	Superficially an inclusive organization, but in reality everything openly discussed is already prepared and decided	Organizations characterized either by authoritarian decision-making (a boss) or paralysis
A high degree of informal discussion and gaining of acceptance	Politicized organization—unpredictable, as proposals and decisions may be changed during negotiations in an ongoing meeting	Decision-making according to Nemawashi—well-analyzed and negotiated decisions enjoying a high level of acceptance once they are formally decided	Depending on the level of activity, the organization may be characterized by either paralysis (no action, only talk) or a type of Nemawashi—analyzed and accepted actions

Our view is that one should aim for somewhere in between: a relatively intense process lasting about a month during which several organizational levels are invited to contribute to the negotiations. Regardless of which start and end dates you set for the process, it is good if the process manager has clear deadlines from the outset. The high level of intensity means that this is a process creating engagement in the organization (remember what we wrote about curiosity about change in Chapter 2). Involving more individuals than just the management team also creates pressure for development in the organization. Furthermore, inclusion facilitates execution and follow-up (i.e., the Kanri part). Once the target condition at an organizational level has been determined, negotiations begin within the respective function to determine which activities at the team and individual level will be carried out to support the overall objective. Ideally, a new year begins with Kanri (i.e., management).

BOX 5.11 NEMAWASHI—UNIQUE BUT NOT REALLY

In their book *The Japanese Mind*, Davies and Ikeno (2002) explore the reasoning on Nemawashi and related concepts, such as Kenkyo (humility), Shudan Ishiki (group awareness) and Uchi to Soto (double meanings). Davies and Ikeno argue that Nemawashi is unique, but not really. There are similar concepts in other cultures. They mention spadework, which is all the work involved in preparing and gaining acceptance before a project gets a green light. In a similar sense, they use the concept skunkwork, meaning the innovation efforts partially carried out in secrecy. In business studies, there is also the concept of muddling through, which was first used in political science to describe how politicians seek to gain acceptance for their ideas before formal decisions are made. Everyday concepts such as politicking and lobbying may also be linked to this phenomenon. According to Davies and Ikeno, Nemawashi differs from several of these concepts in some respects:

- Decisions are often made in Japan by means of consensus (i.e., everyone agrees when the decision is made). Even if the manager enjoys significant decision-making power, employees can nevertheless easily sabotage the decision if they don't agree with it. Hence, it is important for the manager to gain acceptance for their proposals well before decisions are made.
- Decisions in Japan are often made before they are formally decided in formal meetings. This is done so that no one will lose face in an open discussion. Formal meetings are thus more ceremonial in nature.
- Nemawashi seeks to inform, reason and informally negotiate. It is not about promoting and "selling" your proposal. So, what we frequently refer to as lobbying for a particular idea is not the same as Nemawashi.

BOX 5.12 WANT TO LEARN MORE?

Many people have been fascinated by Japanese culture, not least since it represents an important element in Japanese production philosophies. In this chapter, we have discussed Nemawashi, the "Japanese form of interpersonal communication," a definition we have taken from Saito (1982). We have also used Davies and Ikeno's (2002) accessible book on Nemawashi and related concepts.

- Saito, M. (1982), Nemawashi: A Japanese form of interpersonal communication. *ETC: A Review of General Semantics*, *39*(3), p. 205–214.
- Davies, R. J. & Ikeno, O. (eds.) (2002), *The Japanese Mind: Understanding Contemporary Japanese Culture.* North Clarendon: Tuttle Publishing.

The management team is in focus in the Hoshin phase. This is quite obvious as this is frequently where strategy work originates. The most comprehensive overview of research on management teams is the following book by Cannella, Finkelstein and Hambrick.

- Cannella, B., Finkelstein, S. & Hambrick, D. C. (2008), *Strategic Leadership: Theory and Research on Executives, Top Management Teams, and Boards.* Oxford: Oxford University Press.

In Box 5.2, we discussed leadership in "good to great" companies. Jim Collins' book, which we referred to, is well worth reading. He has also published additional books (see jimcollins.com) where he develops many interesting principles and concepts.

- Collins, J. (2004), *Good to Great (Why Some Companies Make the Leap and Others Don't).* London: Cornerstone.

In Box 5.4, we used a quote from Mark DeLuzio on the difficulty of focusing. The quote originates from Roy Kesterson's book on Hoshin Kanri. The second part of this book consists of interviews with American experts in Hoshin Kanri. They focus on many of the critical issues arising when introducing Hoshin Kanri.

- Kesterson, R. (2015), *The Basics of Hoshin Kanri.* New York: Productivity Press.

We mentioned earlier that we find the book by Cowley and Domb to be the best work on Hoshin Kanri. In the section "The benefits and advantages of Hoshin Kanri," they summarize the most important things you need to know about Hoshin Kanri.

- Cowley, M. & Domb, E. (1997), *Beyond Strategic Vision: Executive Corporate Action with Hoshin Planning*. Amsterdam: Butterworth-Heinemann Business Books.

Chapter 6

Kanri in Hoshin Kanri

When the New Year bells have stopped ringing, the time has come to execute and follow up on the activities agreed upon in the organization at the end of last year. If the Hoshin phase has been successful, there is now an accepted set of activities to be carried out—activities based on the prioritized challenges that the organization is to manage in the coming year. It is now a matter of these activities being carried out, followed up and becoming the basis for learning.

6.1 The Meaning of Follow-Up

The term *follow-up* is used in two senses in Hoshin Kanri. The first and perhaps most obvious is that activities are being followed up to ensure that they have been carried out. The second meaning, however, is more important. This is also a question of following up in the sense that you ask yourself how things went when the activity was carried out. In hindsight, was the activity relevant for reaching the target condition during the stipulated time? What did we learn when we tried to or did carry it out? What can we take with us to the next year? Were certain elements not adequate? Were other issues identified, issues that should be addressed during the year? Perhaps some activity should be replaced? In other words, this is a type of follow-up inserting flexibility and learning during the execution of Hoshin Kanri. The questions are based on the PDCA methodology (plan, do, check and act/standardize); that is, the same analytical approach forming the structure of the A3.

DOI: 10.4324/9781003194811-6

Ideally, each employee is now the owner of a number of activities, meaning specific objectives and related activities to be carried out during the fiscal year. When these activities are aggregated at the "departmental level," the department's objectives may be achieved. If multiple departments complete their activities, this function will achieve its objective for the year, and if all functions do the same, the organization's objectives for the year will be achieved. In a way, this can be compared to a pyramid: the bottom building blocks determine what the top looks like. It is worth nothing that several people can work on the same activity, while there is always one person owning the activity.

In the previous chapter, we mentioned the possibility of linking Hoshin Kanri to the existing structure for performance reviews. In performance reviews, the focus is typically on the employee's objectives and development, after which it is assumed that this contributes to the organization moving in a satisfactory direction. In Hoshin Kanri, the focus is on the defined activities contributing to the organization achieving its one-year target condition. If it is possible to link the individual's development plan to Hoshin Kanri activities, one may create a leverage effect. What is good for the individual is (almost always) also good for the organization!

Hoshin Kanri may also be linked to the efforts to achieve continuous (daily) improvements. In Chapter 1, we pointed out that Hoshin Kanri and continuous improvement efforts interact in an organization. Hoshin Kanri works with strategy from the top down. Daily improvement efforts distill strategic issues in daily problems from the bottom up. We illustrate this in Figure 6.1.

Another major difference from traditional follow-up is that the "pulse" is crucial in Hoshin Kanri. In order for the organization to receive feedback on whether the direction is the right one and whether the ambitions appear to be realized during the year, regular and frequent feedback from the organization is required. This does not work if, as is often the case, you decide on activities in December and then meet again in October the following year to check on how things went.

In a well-functioning Kanri process, on the contrary, regular follow-up meetings occur at all levels. Frontline managers should meet with their employees on a regular basis to follow up on their activities. Likewise, managers at different levels should meet so that the management team and the CEO may receive a status report on how the strategy is progressing. In line with the earlier discussion, such a status report should describe the current condition in terms of the execution of the decided activities but also include the qualitative element. This enables management to continuously learn about the process and its execution and to add or subtract activities throughout the year.

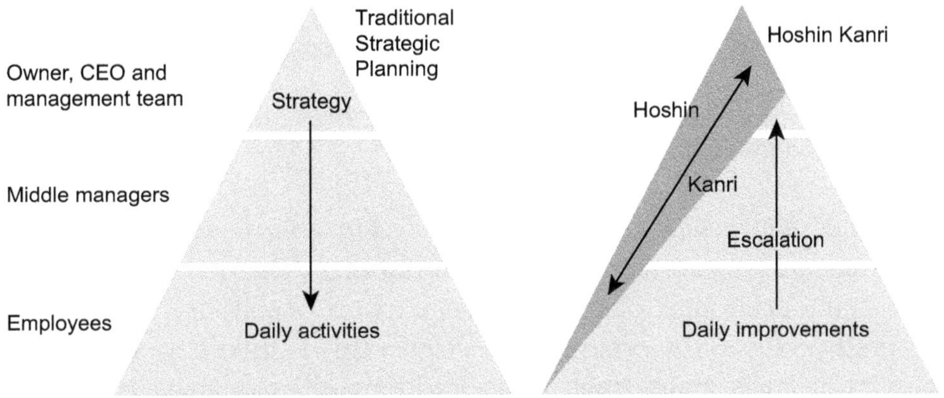

Figure 6.1 The Role of Daily Improvements in Hoshin Kanri

Such a continuous follow-up process, where meetings are dedicated to discussing strategy at all levels of the organization, is essential if Hoshin Kanri is to be successful. We all know that everyday work typically takes over and strategy is prioritized to a lesser extent. If a structure as the one described previously is established, an organizational form of mental pressure materializes. The CEO wants follow-up from the functional managers, which means that they want follow-up from the department managers and so on further down in the organization. At the same time, including employees at lower levels in the organization means that they will ask questions about how work is progressing at levels above their own. This pressure may thus also occur from the bottom up. Overall, there will be an increasing curiosity about the future of the organization. This is a good thing, as we do applaud engagement!

This follow-up can be visualized in several ways. One is to create A3s at different levels, where the top level of the hierarchy is the A3 in which the CEO organizes their follow-up. Another possibility is to use an X-matrix at the management level. A third way is to use a so-called sunburst diagram. In Chapter 7, we describe these analytical tools in more detail. Feel free to also read the case from the Lindbäcks Group on this topic. However, we can't help ourselves from already including a quote here from this case regarding the visualization effect (see Box 6.1).

In Figure 6.2, we have tried to describe the different layers formed by Hoshin Kanri. The outermost layer is the vision describing the direction. In the figure, we have set the time period to three to five years. The vision is the point of departure for identifying major challenges (breakthroughs). This work represents the basis for this year's objectives, which are broken down throughout the organization during the Hoshin process while also

BOX 6.1 THE LOGIC IS ENGAGING!

Stefan Lindbäck, CEO of Lindbäcks Bygg, says the following about visualization by means of sunburst diagrams:

> Things get easier for me as CEO as I'm able to explain how things are related. The board (the sunburst diagram) hangs outside the door here. There, we may explain why it's important to build projects in Gothenburg. Because this is linked to a strategic objective stating that we should have this capacity in three years' time, which means that we have to start sooner or later. The logic is strong, transparent and understandable. We have hired a large number of people in the last two years. Unless we open up as to why you should work with us and what the objective is, they quickly move on. We have to ask them for a dance. That means that we actually have to let the individual join in and poke around. Then they understand and are engaged. Then you get this feeling of "Yes, this is where I want to work!"

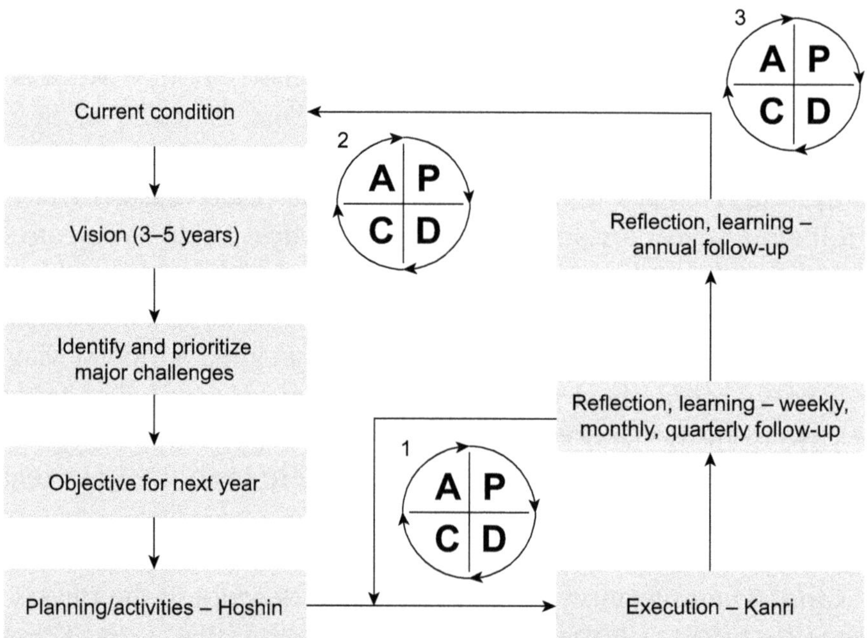

Figure 6.2 Hoshin and Kanri over a Three- to Five-Year Cycle (Partially based on Dennis 2006 p. 128)

being linked to activities. This is the subject of the internal "negotiations" we discussed in Chapter 5. The activities are carried out during the fiscal year, followed up regularly and communicated (spinner 1). At the end of the year, an overall follow-up is carried out, which is then communicated and compared to the original description of the current condition. Perhaps something needs to be revised, and perhaps the vision also needs to be tweaked somewhat (spinner 2). So, you keep using spinner 1 for one more year. After two to three spins, it is time for a more substantial analysis of the current condition and vision. Perhaps it is time for clearly revising or rewriting the vision (spinner 3).

6.2 Catchball

As we hope has been shown by now, Hoshin Kanri sets out to link challenges to objectives, which are then linked to activities, which are then at the next level translated into new challenges, objectives and (more specific) activities—and so on through the organizational hierarchy. This is a two-way process, where you first negotiate through the different levels of the organization to identify and determine activities for everyone, followed by executing, following up and evaluating activities and the entire process.

This approach for spreading a message is in Hoshin Kanri referred to as catchball. In this context, it is about discussing challenges, negotiating (in a positive sense) objectives and reporting outcomes. In other words, it is a "back-and-forth" process. You can "catchball" in many different ways. Many people do so intuitively and integrate it into their leadership style.

However, the point of Hoshin Kanri is that a standardized approach is created that is then applied throughout the organization. In Section 2.1.4, we argued that standardization is a prerequisite for developing the organization. The reason is that not standardizing the work processes makes it difficult to understand the current condition. And, if you don't understand the current condition, it will be difficult to set new objectives and determine how to get there. However, catchball is linked to all seven principles. Two of the most obvious links are found in relation to the principle of "managing by learning" described in Section 2.1.6, where we discussed the need for transformational leadership, and to the principle of "facts drive and decide" in Section 2.1.7, where we emphasized focusing on facts in decision-making processes. Both of these principles are essential for the catchball process to work.

Earlier, we wrote that catchball is about discussing challenges, negotiating in a positive sense of the word. This suggests that challenges can be discussed in several ways. A common approach, for example, is to pass the buck, which means that the objective of the negotiation is to make things as easy as possible for your own department or you as a manager. In Hoshin Kanri (and lean management), coaching leadership aims to create a positive atmosphere regarding these negotiations.

6.3 Coaching Leadership According to the Kata Philosophy

The "Japanese wonder," often exemplified by the success of Toyota, has been studied extensively. In recent years, however, there has been an increasing focus in these studies on the "soft" factors. The focus has been directed toward the particular culture of Toyota. An influential book focusing on soft factors is Mike Rother's *Toyota Kata* (2009). Just like so many other Japanese words, Kata is difficult to translate, but Rother describes it as a pattern of thinking and conducting oneself that is practiced over and over every day at Toyota (p. xvi), a kind of consistent role modeling.

Rother's message is that the success of Toyota and thus the entire lean movement is not about techniques and different analytical tools but concerns how employees think and behave when working with challenges. The point of departure is that if you continuously develop the way employees think and behave, they will apply techniques and working methods in an efficient manner. This message means that one crucial task is to coach employees to think according to the scientific systematic approach we discussed in Chapter 1. This will create a common approach with regard to challenges. This approach is entirely in line with how we perceive coaching in Hoshin Kanri and can be summarized in a poem by Søren Kierkegaard (see Box 6.2).

We want to highlight three sections in the poem. The first is about finding the person to coach where this person is located. The second is about knowledge and the third is about power. Together, the message in these passages forms the basis for effective coaching in terms of applying the scientific approach.

6.3.1 Finding the Employee Where They Are Located and Starting There

It may seem obvious that you need to understand the individual to be coached before initiating the coaching process. Unfortunately, this is not always the case. In Hoshin Kanri, however, this statement means a bit more than that. In line with the scientific systematic approach, it is essential to analyze and understand the current condition. When it comes to coaching, the "current condition" is the situation in which the individual to be coached is located. What does this individual know? Which experiences does the employee carry with them? Which are the employee's ambitions? What does the employee want to accomplish? What pressure is the employee under? The answers to questions such as these offer knowledge regarding the current condition and the basis for coaching.

In addition, there is always a situation that needs to be analyzed. Why should the employee be coached? What is the target condition of coaching? Are there multiple target conditions?

BOX 6.2 THE FOUNDATION OF COACHING

Søren Kierkegaard is probably the most influential philosopher in the Nordics. He lived in Copenhagen in 1813–1855 and was best known for basing his philosophy on the individual's perceived truths, which was a radical notion at the time. What is true for an individual at a specific point in time guides their thoughts and behavior. This is expressed very strikingly in the following well-known poem, which is familiar in many professions.

> *If One Is Truly to Succeed in Leading a Person to a Specific Place, One Must First and Foremost Take Care to Find Him Where He Is and Begin There.*
>
> *This is the secret in the entire art of helping. Anyone who cannot do this is himself under a delusion if he thinks he is able to help someone else.*
>
> *In order truly to help someone else, I must understand more than he—but certainly first and foremost understand what he understands. If I do not do that, then my greater understanding does not help him at all.*

> *If I nevertheless want to assert my greater understanding, then it is because I am vain or proud, then basically instead of benefiting him I really want to be admired by him.*
>
> *In all true helping the helper must first humble himself under the person he wants to help and thereby understand that to help is not to dominate but to serve, that to help is a willingness for the time being to put up with being in the wrong and not understanding what the other understands.*

English translation by Hong, H. V. & Hong, E. H. (1998), *The Point of View for My Work as an Author.* Chapter IA, §2, p. 45. Princeton: Princeton University Press.

6.3.2 Understand More Than the Employee Does—But First Understand What They Understand

Understanding more than the employee does concerns expertise, meaning knowledge of the issue addressed in the coaching in this particular case. Coaching in itself is a technique that is important to be familiar with—in fact, ideally everyone in the organization should be

BOX 6.3 COACHING CONVERSATIONS

At the Lindbäcks Group, they have started using what they refer to as employee pulse, a kind of coaching conversation where they "take the pulse" on the employees. Once fully implemented, the goal is to establish a continuous dialogue with employees to ensure that they are on the right track with regard to the development of both the company and the individual. The aim is to focus on the "here and now" in relation to a future state. Stefan Lindbäck, CEO of Lindbäcks Bygg, discusses the notion:

> Let's say you are managing a team of eight people. You schedule 20 minutes every Friday for employee pulse. Meaning that the leader meets the same person every eight weeks. In these conversations, you sit down at a scheduled meeting

and discuss the individual in question—challenges at home or other aspects that feel important. No meeting minutes, it is about setting aside 20 minutes where the employee is in focus. If you have done it a few times with each individual, you don't need a schedule, it just keeps on going. Then you have a rich conversation. When you then carry out the annual performance review, things will be so much easier. That is just what my dad did—he was present everywhere. He talked to everyone and made everyone feel as if they were seen. There was moose hunting and children and relatives here and there. You then create the kind of trust that makes people want to go to work—a sense of that it is important that I go to work because I have value as an individual. I'm seen and listened to. The aim is now for us to do this more systematically. We have just started to introduce it. We have four management levels. It's tough. That is why we need to organize leadership in a way enabling you to cope.

able to coach each other according to the Kata technique. However, this doesn't mean that there is no need for knowledge on the issue that is the topic of the coaching. Being proficient in the Kata technique reduces the need for expertise but can't entirely replace it. How else can you coach in the right direction?

Nevertheless, the second part of the sentence is at least as important. Having expertise with regard to the challenge and the area in which the employee works can turn you into an expert. However, the feeling of being an "expert" in a specific area may be misleading. It could result in you finding something easy, thus moving along too quickly in your coaching. To be a good coach, you must be able to balance your "expert knowledge" in the subject area with the level of knowledge of the person being coached. Don't forget the goal of coaching. You are not the one who should shine, your employee should.

Sometimes, simple things remind you of the goal of coaching. In the example in Box 6.4, we describe how the coaches were reminded of the principles of Kata coaching through a "simple question" that ended up changing the entire course of events. One can't help to wonder what would have happened had it not been asked.

BOX 6.4 "WHAT DOES THE WORD VISION MEAN?"

The workshop had not been in progress for all that long before we realized that it didn't work. The four members of the management team started to fidget already at an early stage, and it was clear they wanted to be somewhere else. They simply didn't understand the point of mapping out the market and analyzing their current condition in order to formulate a vision for the future of the company. It was too far from their daily work. This became clear when one of them simply asked, "What does the word vision mean?"

Over a cup of coffee, we who managed the workshop changed our tactics and decided to carry out an experiment. After the break, the workshop instructor asked the participants what constituted their greatest challenge at this particular moment. It turned out that they were facing major changes with regard to energy supply. Should they invest in a new boiler and thus also in new machines affected by the choice of energy system? The municipality were eager to know what they intended to do.

A decision was immediately made to put aside the overall efforts to create a vision with all the subsequent analyses of what it would entail to instead tackle the urgent challenge facing the company. This perked up the participants. Now, we discussed something concrete and "important." The workshop instructor led the conversation and asked "why" probably more than a hundred times. All answers helped to finish the jigsaw puzzle.

6.3.3 Helping Is Not Wanting to Rule But Wanting to Serve

Ruling is a strong word. Most people involved in coaching will probably not think of the word rule in relation to this process. Unfortunately, however, this is often what we do. We use the word "we" as this also happens to us, all the time. Perhaps even in this book? Let us explain further. "Rule" is what you do when you take a shortcut and tell the conclusions to the person you are coaching, thus not giving this person time to arrive at an insight themselves. You have probably also been a little frustrated at some point, and instead of waiting for the person in question, you have proposed a solution. Well, that is ruling. In this situation, you are the expert coming up with the expert solution. You have thus completely missed the point. Your job as a coach is to (a) develop the insights of the one being coached as to how to solve challenges and (b) create curiosity in the one being coached so that they continue to solve new challenges by themselves. In other words, it is about getting the employee to grow mentally. Solving the specific challenge the employee is currently working on is actually secondary.

We now refer to a situation where the coach and the person being coached work practically with a challenge that is real but perhaps not urgent. When things are urgent, perhaps you act somewhat differently. Then you may have to intervene first and coach later. A classic example is a child who is about to put their hand on a hot stove. Most likely no parents would start coaching the child at that point; instead, we react instinctively based on our expertise that a hot stove equals a risk of burning your hand.

The difference between a more "ruling" attitude and coaching is in this case found after the event. You can either choose to introduce a rule, a ban followed by harsh words, or sit down and together with your child analyze what happened so that the two of you can both learn how to avoid a similar situation in the future. Perhaps you should even carry out a controlled experiment to help your child become more familiar with similar situations in the future.

6.4 Encouraging Learning and Development by Experimenting

The goal of coaching is to encourage learning with regard to how to solve challenges. This means that the primary purpose is not to solve the current challenge. In essence, this is about getting the one being coached to reflect and analyze. If they learn how to do this, they are prepared for future challenges. If you simply solve the current challenge, chances are that it will eventually return. As we pointed out previously, it is crucial that you avoid shortcuts by offering answers. This is always about encouraging the one being coached to themselves come up with solutions. The Kata methodology suggests some questions that may serve as a point of departure:

- Which challenge are you trying to solve and why?
- What is your target condition?
- What is your current condition?
- What was your last experiment?
- What was the outcome?

- What did you learn?
- What will be your next experiment?
- What do you think will happen? Results? Lessons?
- When can I come and see what you learned?

As you can see, the focus is on the experiment. Experimenting is about learning by doing. This creates practical knowledge, unlike the kind of theoretical knowledge in which you know what to do but have not practiced the solution. In his book, Mike Rother (2009) stresses that there are no failed experiments, as experiments exist to create insights enabling you to design a better experiment the next time. But as we discussed in Section 2.2, experiments must be planned to secure a valuable learning. Doing things without an analysis of current conditions or a defined target condition is not providing an opportunity for learning. It is just a waste of time.

We have now talked a lot about how a coach coaches people. But who coaches the coach? Most likely you, our reader, are one of those who will coach others. In such a case, however, not only do you need to learn the technique we discuss here—it is also important that you *develop* your practical coaching skills. This is partially a matter of attitude. If you look upon each coaching session as an experiment, you can also evaluate the experiment, reflect, learn and standardize new knowledge that will hopefully lead to your coaching improving by the next time (i.e., in the next experiment). In such a learning process, it is important that you and the person you coach stop at regular intervals and evaluate how you interact. If you also use a mentor who coaches you in terms of developing your coaching, this may create a basis for increased learning. Perhaps we may talk about first-order learning, in which you learn the actual coaching technique, and second-order learning, in which you use an external mentor who can help you reflect upon more fundamental issues.

We discuss experiments in more detail in Sections 7.4 and 7.6. Experimenting is a cornerstone of the scientific approach forming the basis of Hoshin Kanri.

A final point is that pace is important. When Kata coaching, we should focus on target conditions that are close in time. A good experiment should perhaps take a week or less to conduct, so weekly or at the most two-week intervals between coaching sessions is our recommendation. This to achieve a good learning effect on the coaching technique, but also to achieve a good effect in the change project that is in focus.

BOX 6.5 TRIAD COACHING

In our courses, we have experimented with some aspects of coaching. One approach we like and now frequently apply is the following: everyone in a group gets the same task for the next session. When the group meets, the participants are separated into triads and have the coaching questions in front of them. They then sit down by themselves, and participant A starts to coach participant B in the task everyone was given. Participant C sits quietly, observes and takes notes. After about 15 minutes, participant C stops the coaching and gives feedback for five minutes to participants A and B. Then, participant B coaches participant C, with participant A as an observer, followed by, finally, participant C coaching participant A with participant B as an observer. In three times 20 minutes, all participants have thus had all the roles in the triad. We then conclude with a 20-minute joint session to together reflect upon the coaching process. We think that this total of about 80 minutes is time well spent. If you want to, you can continue with a new round but in different triads. Alternatively, the meeting breaks up and you meet again for a new round after a suitable amount of time has passed. If this is successful, it is a form of training in which you can also address a strategic challenge. Killing two birds with one stone!

6.5 Alternatives to Hoshin Kanri According to the Toyota Model

In this chapter we have followed the structure forming the basis of the bulk of the Hoshin Kanri literature: an annual cycle consisting of Hoshin (planning) and Kanri (management), where the goal is that the entire organization should be involved in the strategy work by all employees participating in planning and carrying out activities and where you use a design of the process that follows the established organizational chart.

However, in many of the organizations we have encountered, reality looks quite different. One reason for this may obviously be that they are undergoing development—for example, they may be introducing Hoshin Kanri and find themselves in one of the steps we describe in Chapter 4. It may also be that operations are organized in an unusual way. For instance, a company we presently work with has not included all functional heads in the management team, and instead they have included some experts from lower levels in the organization. This possessed a challenge when organizing the Hoshin Kanri process.

However, departing from the Toyota model may also be a more conscious decision. There is no way for us to determine whether "our" model is the best or whether another variant is more effective. What we can do is to discuss some variants and their pros and cons.

Let us start with the latter point. Do the Hoshin Kanri efforts follow the established organizational structure? The seemingly simple approach we have described is to follow the organizational chart and assume that the existing management team constitutes the core of the strategy work. As we have described so far, the Hoshin process is then channeled based on the organizational structure, typically according to the organization's *functions*. The advantage of this way of organizing is obvious, since responsibility for strategy work coincides with operational responsibility in the organization. If you are responsible for production, it is quite natural that you are also responsible for strategically developing production.

We touched upon the downside of this solution in Section 5.4 when we discussed the need to focus on a small number of challenges. The point was that focusing on a few major challenges means that functions need to cooperate. Otherwise, function-based thinking will just get worse. Just to exemplify, if the challenge facing the head of production is increased customer satisfaction instead of "developing production," we then encourage organizational transparency.

Another way of organizing Hoshin Kanri is to start with *challenges* instead of functions and create a project team for these, either a project team for each of these challenges or a project team for the entire Hoshin Kanri process. An obvious advantage of this way of organizing is that it opens up the teams in terms of composition. Individuals may be included depending on their expertise, personality traits and/or their potential significance with regard to the challenge in focus. Depending on the nature of the challenge, one may also choose how much of the organization to involve in the strategy work. As challenges are addressed, the composition of the project teams may also change. This makes the process more dynamic, and the work becomes more flexible. An example of this could be to initiate strategic development work on sustainability. Sustainability is a challenge that invites all functions to participate. It is open for interpretation but at the same time clear in direction. And there certainly will be engagement!

A drawback of this approach is that it is demanding. For example, it is not possible to use the standard reporting structure; instead, new types of meetings with new constellations are required for reporting on how the work is progressing. Management also needs to apply a great deal of focus, or else there is a risk that strategy work is not prioritized. According to Hoshin Kanri, one of the points of strategy work is to create a clearer sense of ownership of the strategic issues and their solutions. It would be a pity if this point were lost. A further challenge with this challenge-based way of working is the risk that the development work will be project oriented. When the challenge "is solved," the conquered ground will be lost as attention shifts to a new challenge.

Danaher's model is somewhat of a compromise between the prior two models. Danaher is an American conglomerate often used as an example when discussing Hoshin Kanri. So-called Kaizen events are an important element in their strategy work. The basis of this model is a Hoshin process (they refer to it as policy deployment) in which the management teams in the various companies in the group identify and negotiate the major challenges and related objectives (they use the term breakthroughs). The management (Kanri) differs from our model, as Danaher works with Kaizen, which is a familiar concept in lean management. It is frequently translated as "continuous improvements" and refers to modifications made more or less on a daily basis to improve the current process. These types of Kaizen activities may be described as "maintenance Kaizen" (the same term used by Liker & Hoseus 2008 p. 177). Danaher also works with this type of Kaizen but refers to this as daily improvements. The opposite of maintenance Kaizen is so-called Kaikaku events, which focus on radical and fundamental changes, often of a production system. According to Danaher, Kaizen events can be said to exist in between these two alternatives.

Based on the major challenges identified in Danaher's Hoshin process, several Kaizen events are organized throughout the year. At a Danaher company we visited, five to ten individuals have attended 30 to 40 different Kaizen events per year. An event takes three to five days to carry out. If they are well prepared, they only take three days. In total, approximately one thousand working days are each year invested in development efforts based on the Kaizen event methodology. The first day is a start-up day in which the methodology is repeated and trained. The second day focuses on the current condition and on brainstorming solutions. The third and fourth days focus on implementing and testing solutions, while on the fifth day, a final solution is evaluated and selected, which is then decided to be the new standard. Follow-up takes place after 7, 14, 30, 60 and 90 days.[1]

The Kaizen event format makes it beneficial to address fairly well-defined issues concerning one aspect of the organization's major challenges. This also means that the group selected for a specific Kaizen event is relatively limited.

Danaher is quite unique in starting with the identified major challenges when deciding upon the focus of their Kaizen events. It is much more common that Kaizen events are used as a means of accelerating the continuous improvement efforts (maintenance Kaizen).

BOX 6.6 WANT TO LEARN MORE?

Are you looking for a deeper understanding of Hoshin Kanri? Joel Jolayemi has conducted a literature review in an informative way describing the basics of the Hoshin Kanri process:

- Jolayemi, J. K. (2008), Hoshin Kanri and Hoshin process: A review and literature survey. *Total Quality Management, 19*(3), p. 295–320.

Coaching is a broad area with many different points of entry. We have chosen the Kata approach in this book. If you also choose this approach, we recommend Mike Rother's books.

- Rother, M. (2009), *Toyota Kata: Managing People for Improvement, Adaptiveness and Superior Results.* New York: McGraw-Hill.

The focus on learning and dissemination of knowledge represent two of the basic pillars of Hoshin Kanri. Thomas Jackson has created a way of evaluating management systems in which he specifically addresses what he calls president's diagnosis (PD) during the check phase. Jackson here refers to the annual review of how the strategic management system has progressed, in this case Hoshin Kanri. Note that his focus is not on the organization's performance but on the status of the process (management system).

- Jackson, T. (2006), *Hoshin Kanri for the Lean Enterprise: Developing Competitive Capabilities and Managing Profit.* New York: Productivity Press.

Note

1. This information comes from the Danaher Company mentioned earlier. They didn't know whether exactly the same scope was applied in other Danaher companies as well. However, the concept is standardized.

Chapter 7

Extended Discussion and Analytical Tools

When we started to get interested in Hoshin Kanri quite a number of years ago, we bought an introductory book. It was a thick book and we naively and unfortunately thought that the number of pages was related to the amount of wisdom in the book. It turned out that what was interesting in the book didn't take up more than 15 to 20 pages. The rest consisted of a long review of analytical tools that could be applied in Hoshin Kanri but were generic in nature and very familiar in the broader literature on quality and lean efforts.

We later learned that the focus on analytical tools represents a dividing line. Some consultants and books focus heavily on the tools, while others focus on the principles. As you have probably figured out after reading this far, we believe that the focus should be on the principles. That is why we have devoted more than a hundred pages to discussing principles and why we have waited until now to discuss analytical tools in more detail. However, this position does not mean that we consider the analytical tools insignificant. Not at all. If these tools are adopted to the principles and used systematically, they play a crucial role in Hoshin Kanri.

We have selected a few analytical tools that we present in quite some detail. The reason is that we think that it is better if you learn how to apply a few tools in line with the Hoshin Kanri principles than if you know a large number of generic tools. The basic notion in Hoshin Kanri is that many people (the entire organization) should be experts in creating and executing a superior strategy; therefore, it is also a point in delimiting the number of tools. Better that many in the organization are familiar with a

DOI: 10.4324/9781003194811-7

limited number of tools. In Section 7.1, we begin with some tools primarily focusing on the current condition, after which we move on to the future direction (vision) in Section 7.2. After that, we discuss the two process tools PDCA and the A3 in Sections 7.3–7.5. In connection with this, we take a closer look at systematic root cause analysis in Section 7.6 and information aspects in Section 7.7.

7.1 Current Condition

In many places in the book, we have discussed the importance of thoroughly analyzing the current condition before moving on to setting objectives or formulating a vision. However, we have not allocated much space to discussing *how* to analyze and describe the organization's current condition. Such an analysis is important for two reasons. The first is obvious: analyzing the current condition is the basis for identifying the major challenges and formulating the one-year objective. The second reason is that not only management has to determine the current condition for the organization's vision. There is also a need to analyze the current condition further down in the organization. Once management in the Hoshin phase passes the ball and when negotiation begins with the next level in the organization (e.g., the functional level), the employees in the functions obviously also need to analyze the current condition in terms of their particular function being able to meet management's expectations. Hence, it is important that each level in the organization involved in the strategy work is able to perform its own analysis of their current conditions.

We have already introduced a tool for analyzing the current condition: the Readiness Analysis. However, this concerned the current condition with regard to a distinct process: strategy work. The tools we introduce here adopt a broader perspective and can be applied to both specific processes and different units in the entire organization.

7.1.1 SWOT—Framework for Analyzing the Current Condition

SWOT (strengths, weaknesses, opportunities and threats) is the most popular analytical tool in business administration, perhaps since it is often used as an easy way of organizing the results of a brainstorming session. Nothing is wrong with that, but we believe that there are better ways of using the SWOT methodology.

Why perform a SWOT analysis? We have identified three answers to this question:

- Through these four categories, you open up for identifying all forces—both internal and external—affecting the organization. It helps you create an overall list of everything affecting the way the organization develops.
- It is possible to prioritize between different forces having an impact. By placing them in four categories, it is possible to decide which are the most important in each category.
- The process of identifying forces also enables you to ask which forces have an impact today but perhaps not tomorrow. Or vice versa!

So, who performs this analysis? Based on the Hoshin Kanri principles, the answer is simple: everyone involved in the strategy work. Either an individual performs the analysis and then discusses it with and gains acceptance from important stakeholders or the analysis is carried out as a group process. The point is that the quality of the analysis is not given by the analysis itself but is largely determined by the participation in the analysis work. It is about creating a common picture of the current condition, a picture that everyone agrees on and can use as a basis in the subsequent process of establishing the vision and direction of the organization.

As we have pointed out in many places in this book, it is important that everyone shares the same perception of the current condition. If, for example, a management team does not agree on what the current condition looks like, it may be quite difficult to discuss ambitions for the future. One might even venture to say that it is more important to agree on the current condition than to have the current condition be an absolutely correct representation of the state of affairs. In Box 7.1, we describe the importance of agreeing on a current condition that is actually inaccurate.

BOX 7.1 HOPE IS OUR FRIEND!

In extreme cold, the Hungarian pluton on reconnaissance in the Alps had looked for their camp for a long time. The soldiers remaining in the camp increasingly started to fear what had happened to the platoon, but just when they had run out of hope, the platoon wandered in. Against all odds, they had found the way back to the camp. The camp commander carefully listened to their account of what had happened. "We had been lost for a long time and we had given in to fatigue. We had arrived at a situation where we started to take out everything we had to build a shelter. That is when the platoon commander found an old map in his backpack. Suddenly, we had hope! However, a snowstorm was still raging, so we decided to continue building the shelter. But as soon as the snowstorm was over, we took out the map and got our bearings. We saw that if we followed the stream right next to us, we would get to settled areas. And now we're finally here!" After listening, the commander grabbed the old map and looked at it, first with curiosity and then with great surprise. The map was not over the Alps, it was over the Pyrenees.

What had actually happened? After asking some additional questions, it became clear that the platoon had tried several different paths. Eventually, the men started to lose confidence in the platoon commander and they started arguing. When the map was found, there was hope that they would agree on a path. The map showed that if you looked for a valley and followed a stream further down, you would eventually come to a settled area. This is not unique to the Alps; it basically applies to all mountainous areas, including the Pyrenees. (Freely based on Weick 1995 p. 54.)

Let us now move on and start with the first point when analyzing the current condition; in other words, identifying potential forces that affect the organization. Here, it is typically easier to begin with the external forces. Which threats and opportunities exist in the current environment? Are there any trends that could affect our organization in the near term?

7.1.2 PESTEL

A PESTEL analysis represents a good start for identifying the most important trends in the external environment. PESTEL—an acronym for political, economic, sociocultural, technological, environmental and legal—is a tool offering guidance by describing different areas in which important trends can be identified. What matters in the analysis, however, are not the actual trends, as there are so many trends that it is impossible to cover them all. What matters is that you analyze the trends that may constitute forces affecting your organization. If, for example, the price of oil goes up by 50 percent due to political turbulence, will this affect your organization? Will it affect your organization more than it affects your direct competitors? If so, does political turbulence qualify as an important force to include in the form of a threat in your SWOT? Already at this stage, we see that a SWOT analysis is more complicated than we often think. In order to assess the magnitude of threats or opportunities, you need to relate them to your competitors and your own organization. We present an example of this in Box 7.2.

BOX 7.2 ANALYZING TRENDS IN TWO STEPS

If the trend is that the Swedish krona is dropping in value compared to the euro, is this a trend that may be interpreted as an important force for our organization?

In an organization we analyzed, the answer to this question was an immediate no. As it were, the organization didn't export anything. When we continued the analysis, however, the answer changed. We were then told that two large competitors with a large portion of their production in Sweden exported a great deal to the euro area. If the Swedish krona was weakened, there was a possibility that they would sell more abroad, which, in turn, would affect the competition in the Swedish market.

After a more qualified analysis, it was concluded that a seemingly less important trend could represent a positive force for the organization we were analyzing. An important conclusion in this analysis was that in the future, the organization needed to pay more attention to exchange rates and constantly seek out information on developments related to its competitors' exports. This information might be crucial for the competitive environment in the Swedish market.

The greatest mistake you can make in this phase is thinking that what matters is identifying trends. The more trends that are important based on some kind of societal perspective, the better. This focus often results in a decreased focus on evaluating and assessing trends. Which is a pity, because if a trend that is important in itself doesn't constitute a force affecting the organization in the near future, then it shouldn't be included in a SWOT analysis.

7.1.3 Porter's Five Forces Analysis

SWOT represents a significant simplification, as all external forces are categorized as either threats or opportunities. As discussed earlier, this frequently results in an exclusive focus on broad trends in society, meaning that trends more directly linked to the competitive situation are neglected.

This is where an analysis according to economist Michael Porter's five forces may be useful. This is a complex model, and the analysis will be extensive if you are to perform it according to all the tricks of the trade. But there are some core issues you can start with.

But before we do that, we want to say a few words about the "world of models." They always refer to simplifications. A simplification of the five forces model is that it assumes that an organization operates in *one* industry, which is rarely the case. At the trend level, this typically doesn't represent a problem since most trends are broad and thus important for several related industries. When it comes to the industry analysis, this is much more difficult. We then recommend performing a broader trend analysis of the organization as a whole and specific analyses for the different industries in which it operates.

Now to the core questions:

- What are we competing for?
- Which industry are we analyzing?
- What is the current level of profitability in the industry?

The obvious answer to the first question is profit. The fact that the pursuit of profit maximization is the basis of competition is the point of departure in Porter's model. Nevertheless, other resources can also be the focus of competition. For example, many organizations experience a shortage of different types of labor. The five forces analysis may also be adapted to this market, but let us first proceed with the traditional model.

The second question, which industry is being analyzed, is not always easy to answer. An easy way to get started is to identify competitors according to their industry classification (NAICS in North America and NACE in the EU[1]). A review of competitors according to such a classification may offer a good basis for an internal discussion on the competitive situation. As we all know, however, industrial classifications are a blunt instrument, which means that practical experiences need to be added. Which competitors do you encounter in procurement processes and other direct buying situations? Whom do you encounter at trade shows? One question that may arise in this discussion is the geographical focus. The industry's boundaries do not necessarily equal national boundaries. If you operate a grocery store in Canada but close to the US border, you obviously need to include US grocery stores as competitors in your analysis.

One method of defining the industry and also including a simple analysis of the competitors is to let all participants in the analysis write down the main competitors on post-it notes, followed by asking them to place these notes on an outlined model as shown in Figure 7.1. They are then asked to consider whether these will continue to be the key competitors in the future. If they then identify competitors that may be challengers in the future, they need to add these to the list. In the next step, the participants place "their" competitors in the model.

Once everyone has placed their post-it notes, there will likely be a basis for an interesting discussion on who the competitors are and what their competitive strength looks like today and in the future.

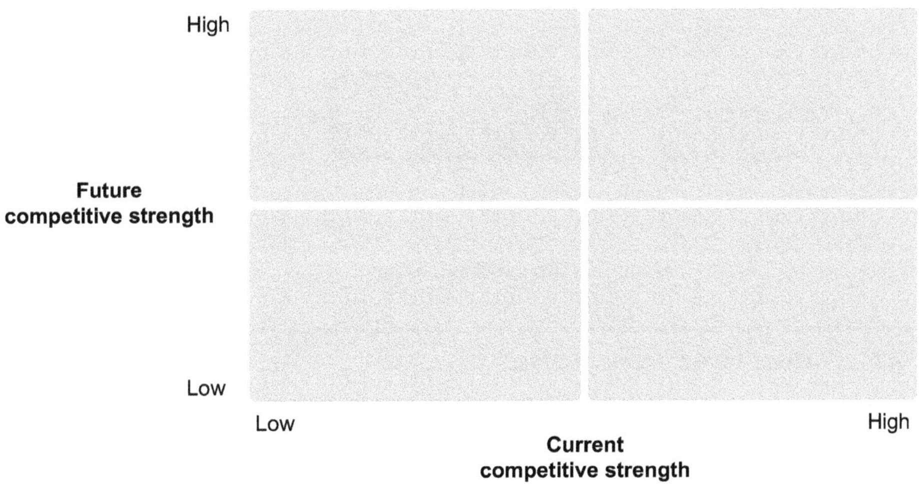

Figure 7.1 Analysis of Competitive Strength

The third question that needs to be asked concerns the profitability of the industry. We know that industries differ in terms of profitability. Many different reviews show different results, but a striking aspect in the ones we have read is that quite significant differences exist between industries (see Box 7.3). Why is that?

BOX 7.3 INDUSTRY-LEVEL PROFIT MARGINS

Numerous lists cover the most (and least) profitable industries. There are some issues with these lists. The two most apparent is that they often constitute a cross-sectional sample and that they neglect fluctuations over time. Furthermore, there is an issue with industry classifications.

Nevertheless, differences between industries are found in terms of profitability. In 2020, IBISWorld published a list of the ten most profitable industries in the United States. Agricultural insurance was at the top with 66.7 percent in profit margin, followed by commercial leasing (47.4 percent). You can find the entire list at www.ibisworld.com/united-states/industry-trends/industries-highest-profit-margin/.

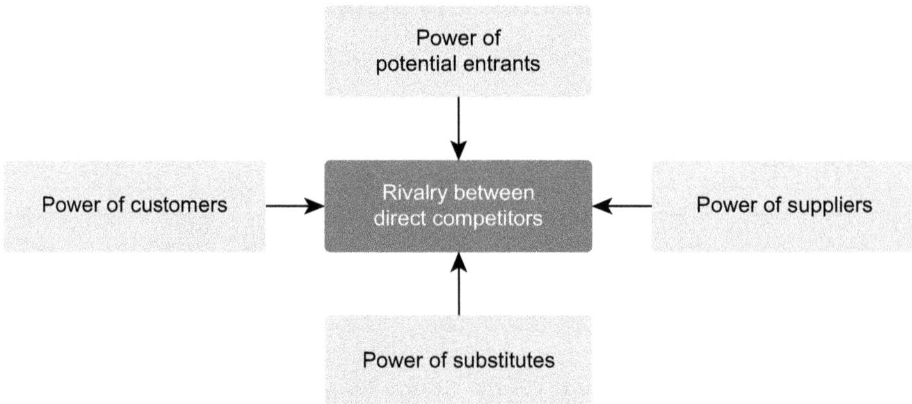

Figure 7.2 Porter's Five Forces Analysis

According to Porter's five forces analysis (Figure 7.2), five factors affect profitability:

- The power of customers
- The power of suppliers
- The power of potential entrants
- The power of substitutes
- The rivalry between direct competitors in the industry

"Power" in this context should be interpreted as the power to keep the profits. If the customers enjoy great power, they keep the money themselves and don't pay all that much for the product. If the suppliers enjoy great power, they charge more. If the rivalry between competitors is high, they collectively give away some of the industry's profits to customers (e.g., through price wars). If the substitutes are competitive, customers will have more options to negotiate between, giving them a good opportunity for negotiating prices. And, finally, if actors not currently in the industry could easily establish themselves and have a major impact on the competitive situation, this could lead to the current actors showing more restraint.

We don't go through these forces in detail; instead, in Table 7.1 we present a battery of 37 questions focused on the relationship between the five forces. Look upon these questions as inspiration. But remember that when you perform a Porter analysis, what you get is a snapshot. Just as in a PESTEL analysis, what matters is what the trends look like. How will power relations between suppliers, industry actors and customers develop in the future? Are there threats or opportunities hidden in that development?

Table 7.1 Questions to Ask in Order to Analyze the Profit Potential in an Industry

Questions to assess the threat from potential entrants
1. Does it take a great deal of investment capital to launch a business in the industry? (Investments in machinery, acquisitions, brand, expertise?)
2. Are operations capital-intensive?
3. How great are the advantages of economies of scale? (In which functions are they the most significant?)
4. Are there limitations with regard to key resources (e.g., access to particular raw materials, patents, markets)?
5. How restrictive are laws and regulations when it comes to launching a new business?
6. How limited is access to distribution channels?
7. How easy is it for customers to switch supplier?
8. What is the significance of customer loyalty?
9. How great is the risk that current actors try to prevent new actors from entering? (Is the industry well organized?)
Questions to assess the power of customers
1. What does the relationship between the customer and supplier structure look like (number of customers/suppliers, size of customers/suppliers)?
2. What is the size of an average order?
3. To what extent is the product/service standardized and interchangeable?
4. To what extent is the product/service strategically important to the customer?
5. Do "symbiotic" production strategies play an important role in the industry (e.g., a "just-in-time" approach)?
6. Is there a risk that a customer will integrate backward and launch a competitive business?

(Continued)

Table 7.1 Continue

Questions to assess the power of suppliers
1. What does the relationship between the supplier and customer structure look like (number of customers/suppliers, size of customers/suppliers)?
2. What is the size of an average order?
3. To what extent is the purchased resource/product/service standardized and interchangeable?
4. To what extent is the product/service strategically important to the supplier?
5. How much would it cost to switch supplier?
6. Do "symbiotic" production strategies play an important role (e.g. production approaches based on customer orders)?
7. Is there a risk that a supplier will integrate forward and launch a competitive business?
Questions to assess the significance of substitutes
1. What does the relationship between the product/service you produce and the substitute look like (quality, function, price)?
2. To what extent are substitutes available on the market?
3. How much would it cost a customer to switch to a competitor/substitute?
4. What do the trends look like? Will the balance between your product/service and the substitute change over time?
Questions to assess the rivalry between existing actors in the industry
1. How many competitors are there?
2. How similar are competitors in terms of size, production, value proposition?
3. Do the strategic objectives of competitors differ?
4. What is the level of capital intensity?
5. Are there clear steps in terms of capacity requiring significant investments?
6. What are the possibilities for differentiation?
7. What does the competitive environment look like (are you "colleagues" or "rivals")?
8. How much and how well do competitors communicate?

9. How strong is the growth in the industry?
10. How significant are the exit barriers?
11. What does access to capital look like for the industry actors? (For instance, are there wealthy owners?)

7.1.4 Internal Environment

So far, we have analyzed threats and opportunities in the external environment. The next step is to analyze the internal environment (i.e., the strengths and weaknesses of the organization). Our impression is that compared to the external forces, this area frequently receives less attention in SWOT analyses. One reason may be that discussing major trends in society is more inspiring, thus neglecting the sometimes sensitive challenges of everyday operations. Another reason may be that it is difficult to determine the scope of the internal analysis. It is easy to get bogged down. Depending on background and training, one may focus on different types of analyses. The basis of many of these is operations management based on resource flows, such as value chain analyses. There is nothing wrong with these in-depth analyses; on the contrary, we too recommend that you in a more thorough analysis use the value chain of your organization as a point of departure. Note that we write "more thorough analysis"—here, however, we remain at an overall level.

You can start by asking yourself what makes your customers buy the company's goods/services. What makes your customers choose your product over that of a competitor at a particular point in time? If you know why, then you know something about your current competitiveness, which is important and constitutes a current strength (as well as, hopefully, in the immediate future). If you (the management team?) perform this analysis and identify the strengths of the organization, it is quite easy to turn the analysis around and ask why some of those you would currently like to have as customers do not buy goods/services from you. This analysis results in the organization's weaknesses.

This kind of analysis is more difficult in the public sector, as the "customer" is frequently not the one paying for the service. Hence, the decision to use the customer as the basis for the analysis easily results in long and complicated discussions on who is actually a customer of the organization. An advantage in the public sector, however, is that there is usually good access to detailed information on resource consumption for comparable organizations. This means that analyzing weaknesses and strengths can be done based on the organization's resource consumption. Areas where you consume fewer resources than comparable organizations indicate that you have a strength, while higher consumption indicates that you have a weakness. So, instead of using the customer as the basis of the analysis, it is thus possible to use units with the same mission as you and that you also have access to information about as a possible point of reference.

Brainstorming a number of reasons why customers choose or do not choose the company's offering is probably not very difficult, but these conclusions are frequently quite superficial and the list can get long. Once you have listed reasons why customers choose or do not choose your offering, these reasons need to be linked to resources controlled by the organization. This is an important step, not least these days as more and more organizations outsource a large number of functions. What if the customers buy your products because they get such good service from your outsourced help-desk in India? Then you have a problem, since this is a resource you don't control.

In Box 7.4, we have listed three possible answers to the question of why customers are buying your products. We have also linked the responses to potential resources. This analysis obviously needs to be deeper. Furthermore, a combination of several different resources frequently explains why customers buy a company's products. Why not make a decision tree listing the resources that contribute to the customer buying your offering? This allows you to identify the resources that seem to be the most important for your organization and that should be analyzed further.

BOX 7.4 WHY DOES THE CUSTOMER BUY?

- The customer buys our products because they have many innovative features. Does the way our research and development is organized represent an important resource?
- The customer buys our products because the price is lower than that of our competitors. Does our efficient production represent an important resource?
- The customer buys our products because they receive excellent service. Does our sales and service staff represent a critical resource?

7.1.5 VRIO

In order to develop the analysis of the identified resources and create consensus, you may use the VRIO tool. VRIO—an acronym for valuable, rare, inimitable and organized—is an analytical tool that enables you to identify the resources and capabilities that are essential to the organization (i.e., what constitutes the strengths and weaknesses of the organization).

The first item in this analysis is to ask whether the resource is valuable. We have already largely answered this question when we focused on the reasons why the customer is buying your offering. But how valuable is the resource? After the initial analysis of the reasons, in this step you should rank which resources are critical, important and less important in terms of the customer's decision.

Let's say that you operate a local pizzeria and that customers present reasons such as proximity, opening hours, service and the crispiness of the pizza crust as reasons for buying pizza from you. These are reasons that can be linked to the geographical location of the pizzeria (proximity), staffing (opening hours), staff (service) and cooking skills (crispiness). Which of these resources is the most important?

The second item concerns rarity. Is this a resource accessible to all competitors or is it unevenly distributed? What does this distribution look like?

If the geographical location of the pizzeria represents a critical resource, how many other pizzerias are there in the same location? If you are the only one in the area, the pizzeria possesses a rare resource. How can you protect it in the best way possible?

The next item concerns whether the competitors can imitate your important resources. In the pizza case, free pizza delivery may pose a major threat to your advantageous location. This represents a way of imitating your location. If home delivery turns out to be a hit, you need to develop another resource to maintain your competitiveness.

The last item, being organized, is quite important since a certain crucial resource has sometimes materialized more by chance and there is no systematic way of maintaining and preserving it in the organization. If this is the case, the resource easily erodes. In the pizza case, both the crispy pizza and the service may be linked to the staff working at the pizzeria. What happens to these resources if the chef and perhaps someone else choose to quit? How are you as the owner/CEO of the pizzeria to reduce this risk and instead preserve the "pizza culture" you seem to have developed? Perhaps by letting the chef become a partner in the business? Perhaps by hiring an apprentice to the chef so that the secrets of the crispiness are disseminated to more people?

After this analysis, we can analyze the permanency of the resources. If one of the critical resources is valuable but not rare or difficult to imitate, then this resource represents a weakness in the organization. It currently plays an important role with regard to your sales, but this is a risky situation. The logic is clear. The more questions that are answered affirmatively (i.e., the resource at hand is rare, difficult to imitate and well maintained by the organization), the more this particular resource qualifies as important for your competitiveness.

7.1.6 SWOT—A Summary

Now that you are about to start summarizing the results of the analysis of the current condition in a SWOT matrix, be careful how you formulate things! The point of the tools we introduced earlier is that the content should be clearly specified (Figure 7.3). No one benefits from a list of strengths including words such as low price, service and flexibility—these tell us very little about the current condition. Be clear and detailed. Also try to put figures on the current condition. How low is your price compared to that of competitors? Is there any way of measuring the level of service? What does flexibility mean to the customers? How does it result in more customers and increased competitiveness? If you are unable to answer these kinds of questions, the analysis of the current condition will be of limited

Figure 7.3 SWOT with Supporting Analytical Tools

value, as this means that you won't be able to assess how things develop. You have not established a clear initial position.

7.1.7 Preparing the Next Step—The Extended SWOT Analysis

Adhering to the systematic analysis, we have until now focused on how to understand the current conditions. In reality, this delimitation is difficult to uphold. It is so easy to be carried away and reflect on the way forward, to reflect on possible solutions. Before we leave this phase, we will therefore introduce an extension to the SWOT analysis that links the analysis of the current conditions to the next phase, where we will entirely focus on the future.

In the extended SWOT analysis, we use the current conditions described in the basic SWOT analysis in a creative way to identify possible ways forward. In the extended analysis, we therefore add a new dimension by cross-tabulating the original factors. As a result, we are no longer *only* identifying threats, weaknesses, opportunities or strengths. We now identify factors that are more qualified. Strengths that also represent an opportunity are really promising. Weaknesses that also represent a threat must be prioritized! And so on.

To illustrate, we build on the pizzeria case introduced in 7.1.5 (the VRIO analysis) where we identified important internal and external factors such as the geographical location of the pizzeria (proximity), staffing (opening hours), staff (service) and cooking skills (crispiness). When teaching the pizzeria case, additional factors as changes in the local demand due to infrastructural changes (new apartment building, new traffic solution, etc.), changes in cultural preferences (increased demand for ready-made food), other cultural changes (increase in neighborhood violence) and the recent pandemic are added.

In Figure 7.4, we have included four or five of these factors in each of the four primary dimensions in the SWOT analysis. When we enter "the extended" version, these factors are the starting point for the creative process to identify possible strategic solutions. An exemplification is Threat 2 (easier to establish a new restaurant), which combined with the conservative style (Weakness 2) and that the pizza chef will retire (Weakness 4) result in the strategic solution to initiate a recruitment of a new chef.

As you see in the extended SWOT, it is the opportunities and threats that drive the strategy development. That is, in this case one starts with the identified opportunities and threats (in the earlier case it was the threat of becoming easier to establish a new restaurant) and match these with the

INTERNAL ENVIRONMENT / EXTERNAL ENVIRONMENT	STRENGTH - Walking distance for many customers (1) - Opening hours good (2) - Customer approach (3) - Pizza crispiness (4) - Long restaurant experience (5)	WEAKNESS - Conservative leadership style (1) - Cost control weak (2) - Employee turn-over increase (3) - Pizza chef retire soon (4) - Boring interior and exterior design (5)
OPPORTUNITY - Building apartment houses close by (1) - Local demand increase (2) - New traffic solution (3) - Ready-made food increase in demand (4)	(1:1-2) Market our advantages, improve capacity, adjust opening hours (3:3,4) Adjust opening hours, improve pizza quality (4:4) Develop the menu	(1,2:3) Employee bonus/shared ownership (1,2,3:5) Major upgrade and capacity increase
THREAT - Pizza home delivery expand (1) - Easier to establish new restaurant (2) - New types of fast food expand (3) - Violence increase (4) - Pandemics increase (5)	(1:1) Walk home delivery (2,3:5) Diversify, new restaurant (4:1,2) Walk home delivery (5:1,2) Walk home delivery	(1:5) Renovate to expand home delivery (2:1,4) Recruit new chef (2,3; 5) Rennovate to modern style (2:2) Purchasing alliance (to cut costs)

Figure 7.4 The Extended SWOT Analysis

internal factors, the existing strengths and weaknesses. But if you prefer to explicitly leverage your existing situation, you can obviously start with the existing strengths (and weaknesses) and match them with appropriate opportunities and threats. In the case presented here, the weakness of low cost control (Weakness 2) is for instance somewhat neglected as the analysis started from the external opportunity and threat side of the matrix.

But it must be underlined once more that the extended SWOT represents a creative exercise, suitable to spur novel ideas. No final decisions should be made at this stage. We return to those decisions in the next phase.

7.2 Vision and Direction

Now that you agree on the current condition, the time has come to focus on the future. In this book, we have discussed objectives in many different ways. We initially discussed the "visionary target condition" for the Hoshin Kanri process in Chapter 2. We described this condition as working according to the seven principles characterizing Hoshin Kanri. We then left the focus on this process to discuss instead in Chapter 5 the vision based on the organization's broader business-related ambitions. At this point, we also discussed the time perspective of the vision (i.e., when the vision should be realized).

Throughout these various discussions, the question has been how to balance guidance and inclusion. Our conclusion in Chapter 2 was that this balance is difficult to achieve since the vision and other objectives should be clear and offer guidance, while at the same time allow for inclusion. In other words, they should enable the employee to make their own analyses and develop their contribution toward realizing them.

In an organization we worked with, we started discussing its vision and overall objectives. The answer we received from the CEO was that the objective was 8 percent EBITDA on turnover (i.e., earnings before interest, taxes, depreciation and amortization). When we received this answer, we felt as if we were in for a true uphill battle. Two problems are associated with this type of objective. The first is that it is not inspiring and engaging for the employees. The second is that it does not in any way offer guidance. After all, 8 percent EBITDA can be achieved in a number of different ways (Figure 7.5).

Inspiration is obviously related to putting things in concrete terms. Finding that it is difficult to grasp what you should achieve means that it will be difficult to be inspired. However, inspiration and engagement are also linked to the purpose. If the manager tells you that your vision is to achieve 8 percent EBITDA on turnover, it is probably not something the people around you would be impressed by, if you even tell anyone about it.

IKEA is often used as an example of a company that is good at describing its vision and target condition. They write the following:

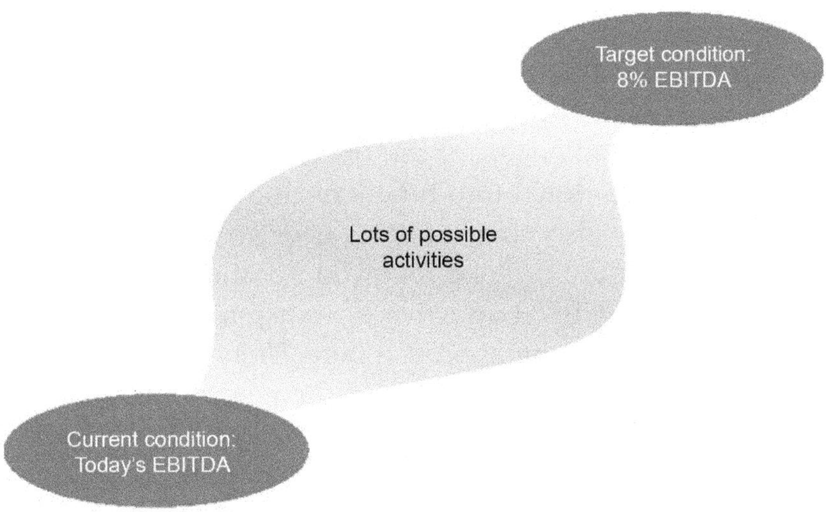

Figure 7.5 An Objective Can Be Achieved in Many Different Ways

> Our vision is to create a better everyday life for the many people—for customers, but also for our co-workers and the people who work at our suppliers.

They present their business idea as:

> to offer a wide range of well-designed, functional home furnishing products at prices so low, that as many people as possible will be able to afford them.[2]

In these two sentences, IKEA describes a vision for the future, a "better everyday life," while offering guidance for how this is to be achieved. They thus offer us both a direction and defined guidance—a good level in terms of concreteness.

Inspiration and engagement can also be related to the challenge as such. If something is difficult and challenging but then presented in a convincing way, it can be very inspiring.

The question of the balance in the vision between being concrete and offering guidance can also be addressed in ways other than formulating the optimal vision. The term "visionary target condition" contains the possibility of separating the more directional element from the more concrete element. The vision, which presents the direction toward a distant future, is combined with a target condition within, for example, three to five years. An advantage of this solution is that the vision can remain "forever," while the target condition is reviewed on a regular basis (e.g., every year or every three years).

As shown previously, the further you move along in the annual Hoshin process, the more concrete the objectives will be. When the vision is translated into annual challenges for the organization and when these are subsequently broken down into functions and departments, then the objectives are obviously also clarified. This is done so that the objectives can be followed up. If they can't be followed up, then you are unable to learn anything about why your activities transpired the way they did. Many managers use the wrong approach here. They believe that the primary purpose of clear objectives is to hold them accountable if these are not achieved. If you are even the slightest bit unsure of your capacity, it is in such a situation easy to formulate somewhat ambiguous objectives that open up for different interpretations when they are to be followed up. This risks leading to a "blame game culture." We argue that the point of departure should be to learn as much from success as from failure. Setting a clear objective and not achieving it, while at the same time being able to learn from this failure, represents a better solution than working with ambiguous objectives.

A good guide on how clear objectives should be designed is the acronym SMART, meaning that an objective should be

- Specific
- Measurable
- Achievable
- Realistic
- Timely

The interesting thing about the SMART model is that it invites people to negotiate regarding the different dimensions. During the process in which the manager and employees negotiate what should be achieved during the year, the SMART criteria can be used as the basis for the contract resulting from the negotiation (see the discussion on inter-level negotiations in

BOX 7.5 WE CHOOSE TO GO TO THE MOON!

An often neglected part of John F. Kennedy's famous 1962 speech about going to the moon concerns the seemingly impossible nature of this vision:

> We choose to go to the Moon! We choose to go to the Moon . . . We choose to go to the Moon in this decade and do the other things, not because they are easy, but because they are hard; because that goal will serve to organize and measure the best of our energies and skills, because that challenge is one that we are willing to accept, one we are unwilling to postpone, and one we intend to win, and the others, too.[3]

In this passage of the speech, Kennedy commits to do everything he can to make this vision a reality. He leads the way, while spurring people's competitive spirit. To set targets in this manner higher than what currently seems possible concerns the vision, but it is also an aspect we touched upon when discussing this year's challenges at the beginning of the Hoshin process (see, for example, Box 5.9 on the challenge of Saab Aerostructures).

Section 5.5). In a basic sense, a contract is an expression that the parties agree on what is to be achieved. This means that an objective considered measurable in one context does not necessarily need to be considered measurable in another context. The same applies to the objective being realistic, clear and challenging. A more definite requirement is that the objective should be specified in terms of timeframe and that someone should be responsible for achieving it. In a way, the same applies in that the objective should be accepted. Unless the employee has "signed" the contract, they have not accepted it. On the other hand, however, such a signature is worthless unless it also means that the employee has understood the objective, accepted it and is mentally committed to working on the objective.

So far, we have presented a number of tools that relate to analyzing the current condition and the vision of the organization. These tools are preferably used in the Hoshin part of the Hoshin Kanri process, which results in this year's activities being identified. In order to create an overview and an ability to follow up in the Kanri part, we need additional analytical tools. We have already touched upon two of these: PDCA and the A3. We now present these tools in more detail.

7.3 PDCA and the Scientific Systematic Approach

To recapitulate, earlier we linked the seven principles characterizing the visionary target condition of an organization working with Hoshin Kanri to a scientific systematic approach. In Section 2.2, we made three assumptions regarding how this approach operates:

- It is a good idea to find out where to go before you start running. Careful consideration pays off in the long run.
- Experiments in the broad sense of the word constitute a way of learning. Unless you experiment systematically, it is difficult to develop practical knowledge.
- The scientific systematic approach benefits from a supportive working process.

In the same section, we also introduced PDCA. There, we pointed out that PDCA is both simple and complex at the same time. The logic of this tool—starting with an analysis, then doing something, following up on what was done and, finally, standardizing the outcome—is quite easy to understand. What is difficult is turning this logic into a fundamental approach in the organization. Then, on several occasions in the book we have returned to PDCA and the scientific approach forming the basis of this tool. We continue to do so, and in the next section on A3s and the X-matrix, you find that the logic in these tools is also based on PDCA.

The conclusion here is that the core of Hoshin Kanri is to create a scientific approach in the organization, an approach thus expressed through the PDCA methodology. So, if you are going to prioritize one of all the suggestions made in this book, it is to practice this approach.

As mentioned in Section 2.2, PDCA stands for plan, do, check and act, but there are a number of alternate names. PDSA (plan, do, study, act/adjust) or OPDCA (observe, plan, do, check, act). Other methods based on the PDCA methodology include DMAIC (define, measure, analyze, improve, control) and LAMDA (look, ask, model, discuss, act).

When you encounter the abbreviation PDCA or any of the variants of this concept, we can bet that there is a circle nearby. The circle signals that the PDCA phases are connected, and in the best of worlds, they are part of an ongoing learning process.

But what do we mean by systematic experiments, which we link to the reasoning on PDCA? We could devote an entire book to analyzing the answers to this question, but we make it easy for ourselves and rely on the *Oxford English Dictionary*, which defines the scientific method as

> a method or procedure that has characterized natural science since the 17th century, consisting in systematic observation, measurement, and *experiment*, and the formulation, testing, and modification of *hypotheses*.
>
> **(emphasis added)**

The keywords in this definition are "systematic observation," "measurement," "experiment," "formulation" and "hypotheses." The point of departure is that we all have hypotheses about how the world operates. Some of these are conscious and some are automatic. The fact that a room is lit up when I press the light switch is an example of an automatic hypothesis on how it works. In most cases, we work with automatic hypotheses, since a conscious process requires a fair bit of effort.[4]

The idea of using the PDCA tool is to highlight the hypothesis and the entire scientific work structure:

1. *Plan.* Formulate the objective, the current condition and a hypothesis on how to achieve the objective.
2. *Do.* Test the hypothesis by means of an experiment.
3. *Check* (follow up). Evaluate the result. What can we learn?
4. *Act* (standardize). Standardize the result and disseminate it.

The idea of "testing the hypothesis by means of an experiment" in Step 2 is to formulate a hypothesis in terms of what needs to be done to solve the challenge. During the P-phase, you may then carry out minor tests of this hypothesis before proceeding. One approach in Hoshin Kanri, which we discussed under the prior heading "Catchball," is to test your hypothesis on the superior who introduced the challenge/activity to you. In such a case, formulating the hypothesis becomes a way of testing whether you have understood the meaning of activities in the same way as your superior has. We would once again like to emphasize the importance of giving the P-phase sufficient time—time to understand the challenge (or activities) as well as possible. Today, so-called 360-analyses are popular.[5] In the P-phase, you perform a 360-analysis of the challenge—"360" in the sense that the challenge is analyzed from all directions. What, in fact, is the problem? However, you also

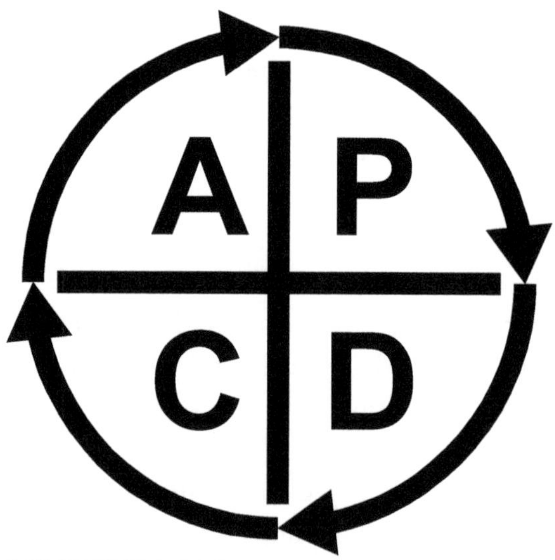

Figure 7.6 The PDCA Phases Are Connected

analyze the current condition, as well as possible solutions and objectives, for instance with the extended SWOT analysis discussed in Section 7.1.7. This will go faster if you do it correctly right from the outset. Remember here the importance of Nemawashi, meaning the need to obtain views and facts as well as to gain acceptance for your analysis, all to create consensus for the next step in the process.

Once a final hypothesis has been formulated, it should be tested in an experiment. In many cases, you only use the term *activity*. However, experiment is a good word since it is important to realize that the activity being carried out is only one of many alternatives for addressing the challenge. Experiments are also linked to evaluation and learning. The idea is to carry out the activity when controlling as many factors possible so that you may then evaluate its impact. If the experiment is unsuccessful, you want to understand why so that you can revise the hypothesis and design a new and improved experiment. If the experiment is successful, you want to understand why so that you can evaluate and learn. This means that follow-up (check) is an important element of the PDCA tool. Similarly, standardization/dissemination (act) is also important. Unless you pay attention to this fourth part of the PDCA tool, you easily forget excellent solutions to recurring challenges, thus having to repeatedly reinvent the wheel. In the following section, we have included some tools supporting PDCA and in particular the root cause analysis in the P-phase.

In conclusion, PDCA represents a systematic and planned way of acting requiring a certain measure of calm. This is illustrated in Box 7.7. Appendix 3 presents an educational summary of the PDCA tool as well as a worksheet you can use when introducing the tool in your organization.

BOX 7.6 ACTIVITIES AND EXPERIMENTS

In our courses, we have had several interesting discussions on the concepts of activities and experiments. We initially used "experiment" as a synonym for "activity," and at that point, the importance of using a parallel term was not significant. Gradually, however, we started to distinguish between the terms activity and experiment. The point is that the organization should carry out a variety of activities, but only some of these are experimental in nature. The aim is obviously that all activities in the long term should be experimental insofar that they can be evaluated and learned from. Presently, however, only some may qualify as experiments. By making this distinction, we want to point out that experiments require a little bit more reflection, are a little bit more uncertain and can fail without it being a catastrophe. On the contrary, you may even learn more from a failed experiment than from a successful one.

This distinction has been well received by several organizations in which management believes that they have found shortcomings in the employees' desire to develop. By emphasizing the experimental in the term experiment, they have been tempted to take some risks and try something slightly outside their comfort zone.

BOX 7.7 KATA IN THE CLASSROOM

In our courses, we have experimented with an exercise illustrating the experimental process. You can find the inspiration for this, developed by Mike Rother, at www.katatogrow.com. This was originally an exercise used by Rother in schools, but it has proved to be applicable in many other contexts. We have simplified it and slightly changed some of the steps in the process. It works great in terms of making participants realize the challenges of performing an effective experiment. In short, this is done as follows.

You start by forming teams of four to six participants, which then appoint someone to take notes and someone to clock them. Each team then gets its own 15-piece jigsaw puzzle. The participants begin by practicing completing the puzzle, thus receiving a baseline time. They then have to decide an objective for the task: how quickly they should be able to finish the puzzle after three to five attempts (the person in charge of the competition decides the number of attempts). This is followed by the subsequent attempts, which include a planning phase, a "placing phase" and an evaluation phase. In all its simplicity, this is an effective task. The competitive spirit quickly materializes, and surprisingly many groups use more time for the final attempts. The difficulty in gathering information and reflecting upon it in an evaluation after a completed attempt also becomes apparent after a while.

7.4 How Did It Go? Follow-Up and Evaluation

The question *how did it go?* frequently asked under the heading "check" in a PDCA analysis is a simple question keeping many people busy. There is even a profession entirely focusing on this question. We are thinking of controllers. The question of how did it go can be asked in many different ways and refer to different things. This question can be asked to demand responsibility, in which case the question really concerns whether activities have been carried out as agreed upon. It may also be asked to check whether more action needs to be taken to achieve the intended effect. Finally, it can be asked because the questioner wants to learn. Depending on how things went, what can we learn so that we may either design a new, better experiment and/or change our current standard/process?

When you have come to this point in the book, it is obvious that the third reason (i.e., the learning perspective) is what we advocate. However, it is obviously also important that progress is made in the organization. No organizations survive exclusively on learning!

With regard to the process in focus in this book (i.e., strategy work), it is striking how little follow-up and evaluation actually takes place. In some cases, strategy days might end with all participants writing down a few comments about the process on post-it notes that are then compiled. It could also be that management looks at these for next year's strategy process. Only rarely, however, is it communicated how this affects next year's approach, which means that if learning occurs, it is not visualized in the organization. At the Lindbäcks Group (see Appendix 1), the strategy process has included an evaluation day when management meets to follow up on both the content (i.e., how well the activities have been carried out during the year) and the working process. This represents an example of the ambition to include a "check" phase in the annual planning process.

However, what is lacking in these examples and in all the literature we have read is systematic evaluations and comparisons between parts of the organization or between different organizations in order to compare the effectiveness of strategy processes. No one seems to know how things differ, why that is the case and what to do about it. We have arrived at some questions that could be asked in such a systematic follow-up (see Box 7.8). You may consider it a first attempt to help you get started. We feel that this is area needs much more knowledge, so feel free to get back to us and discuss your experiences.

BOX 7.8 LIST OF QUESTIONS THAT CAN BE ASKED TO CREATE FACTS ABOUT THE STRATEGY PROCESS

- Are you familiar with and able to state the organization's vision?
- Do you experience that you contribute to the overall vision of your organization in your daily work?
- Does your function (or department) have its own vision (or other long-term objective) linked to the overall vision of the organization?
- Do you experience that you contribute to your function (or department) achieving its overall vision in your daily work?
- Are you involved in your organization's strategy work (regularly, sometimes, never)?
- Do you find your contribution to your organization's strategy work to be valuable?
- To what extent do you believe that the organization is operating according to the following principles? (The respondent is ideally given the opportunity to include comments under each principle.)

  - Long-term thinking
  - Change curiosity
  - Focus
  - Process orientation
  - Visualization
  - Managing by learning
  - Facts that drive and decide

7.5 Communicating PDCA

7.5.1 A3

Have you thought about why you keep records or take notes? The basic reason is obvious. Keeping records serves as support for your memory. However, many people look upon records as something difficult and unnecessary, a waste of time. We don't agree. This is based on three reasons.

The first reason is that when you keep records, you need to pay attention. What is said often sounds very logical and rational when being uttered, but when you write it down, you frequently identify gaps in the reasoning.

Putting it down on paper therefore represents a good way of sharpening the reasoning and making it logical and coherent.

The second reason is that most people are short of time. Without records, there is a great risk that you will need to spend a large part of the next meeting on jointly figuring out what was said at the last meeting. You then need to determine who should have done what, followed by different people having to explain why they didn't do what they didn't remember they were supposed to do. Does this sound familiar?

The third reason, also mentioned previously, is that what is written down may be shared. It is possible to share it in the group, which means in a best-case scenario that you have a common picture of what has been said and that the people with things to do have been reminded of what needs to be done. Furthermore, sharing outside the group is also possible. The message can be disseminated, meaning that you may get additional valuable input.

The A3 offers a systematic approach for recording and communicating the results of a PDCA analysis. As the name indicates, the A3 refers to an A3 sheet of paper. The idea is that the format encourages a clear presentation. You can't be all over the place if you want to include the entire project on an A3—focus is needed! As stated by someone in our research team, "Not everyone wants to read a PhD thesis in order to get to the important point." A drawback with the A3, however, is that it is easy to forget that it takes time to be concise.

The only rule in addition to the fact that the paper used should be in the A3 format is that the content should cover all phases in a PDCA analysis (plan, do, check/follow up and act/standardize).

Figure 7.7 presents an example of a basic design of an A3. The left-hand side of an A3 (the challenge) focuses on analysis and planning, while the right-hand side concerns activities to be performed, follow-up and efforts to ensure that the results live on in the organization.

BOX 7.9 PREPARATIONS

Woodrow Wilson, president of the United States in 1913–1921, allegedly said,

> It depends. If I am to speak ten minutes, I need a week for preparation; if fifteen minutes, three days; if half an hour, two days; if an hour, I am ready now.

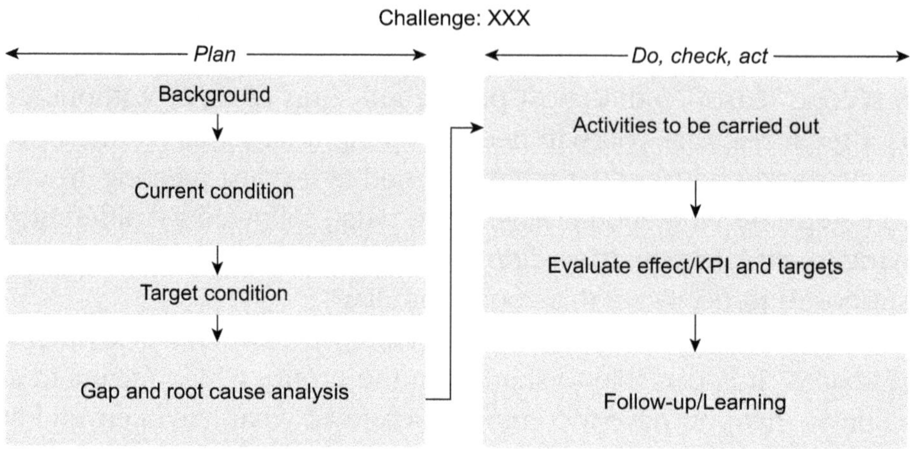

Figure 7.7 A Basic Design of an A3

In the background, you explain the historical context and answer why this issue is important to deal with now. In current conditions, you provide a thorough and convincing explanation of what is happening just now. In this section, you need to be really clear and honest on the present status, even if the current situation is far from how you want it to be. Our experience is that most beginners neglect the necessary investigation needed in this phase, and as a result the presentation here often becomes anecdotal.

In target conditions, you have to communicate a convincing future state and by that answer the question of what life will be like when you reached the future you aim for in this A3 proposal. Obviously, this should be as detailed as possible, but it might be wise to keep it somewhat visionary to secure buy-in from stakeholders and as you return to the more detailed status of the target conditions in the evaluate effect/KPIs and targets section on the right side.

In the gap and root cause analysis, you dig deeper into the challenge. What is preventing you right now from reaching the target condition? Again, here is a need for thorough investigation and well-thought-through presentation of the data. In the activity part, you outline the activities needed to reach the target condition. In many cases beginners tend to fill in this section early in the process, and they then often just list already decided activities. This is a major mistake, because if you don't thoroughly think through what activities are needed and how they are related to the identified challenge, you will waste valuable time and resources.

Finally, two sections are often completely neglected, probably because they are difficult to address, partly due to them being somewhat sensitive to evaluate. If so, we need to remind us that you are not developing this A3 to identify scapegoats. The aim is to develop your processes (see the Hoshin Kanri principles).

In the evaluate effect/KPIs and targets and the follow-up and learning sections, we focus on the learning from your activities. On some homepages, it is argued, "if you can't measure it, you can't improve it." In a somewhat more nuanced way, you could express this as if you are not in agreement on what defines success, you will never agree if you achieved it. However, the key word here is "agreement"; it is not necessarily that you must measure success with a number.

This said, it is vital to reach an agreement among stakeholders on how to define success, and in most cases for pedagogical reasons you will need some indicators. This is just to ensure that you have a productive starting point for learning, a learning that obviously addresses how to solve the focused challenge, but also one on how you could develop your joint knowledge on the current condition and the target condition. It has happened that halfway through the process the owner of the A3 has concluded that the challenge was not really a challenge, as the current condition or target condition was wrongly defined at the beginning!

For the A3 methodology to be successful, it is important that you decide upon *one* approach and seek to apply it consistently. When you become more advanced, at a later stage you may start to introduce different variations of the A3 depending on the task. We have identified three types: a proposal A3, a status review A3 and a problem-solving A3.

- PROPOSAL
  With this A3, you are proposing an action that requires a decision. The gap you identify here is the one between the current condition and the target condition after the action has been implemented. The information you include in this document must be sufficient for achieving consensus on the need (or not) for the action and support you and your stakeholders require to make a good decision on how to proceed if you approve the action. For example, you can use this if you want to propose a bigger investment in the production line or if you are suggesting making changes in the production value stream.
- STATUS REVIEW
  This is an A3 report you normally use during an activity or after an activity is finished to show progress. The gap is defined here as the distance between the plan and the actual status. The purpose of this communication is to identify problems and opportunities that occurred

during the implementation. The A3 should then include proposed actions to correct these deviations.

- PROBLEM SOLVING
  This is probably to most common A3 document—and for many people the A3 report is equal to problem solving. When you are using the A3 for problem solving, you want to clarify the gap—that is, the problem—and recommend potential countermeasures for reaching your target condition. Any countermeasure should be based on a good understanding of the root cause based on facts and data. For example, you might use this approach to overcome problems identified in the daily operation.

In reality, all these types follow the PDCA logic, and what sets them apart is their emphases. The fact that there are different types indicates that there are no specific rules as to how an A3 should be organized. Its appearance should be related to its purpose, hence the different types, but the appearance can also be designed in a unique fashion based on the specific organization. The important thing here is to create a logic that becomes well known and understood in the organization. An established standard enables you to evaluate this very standard and identify opportunities for improvement. The point is that the quality of the A3 is not given by the analysis itself but is largely determined by the participation in the analysis work. You should view the A3 as a tool to engage stakeholders, to create a common picture of your current condition and a basis for subsequent development work. Doing this you should also consider including an analysis of the involved stakeholder when developing the project (and the A3). In the analysis, you can ask such questions as

- What role has the stakeholder in the company? Is it someone who will be responsible for the activity or is it someone that is more distantly connected to the activity?
- What is the level of responsibility? Is it someone from the management team or is your stakeholder an expert or a specialist?
- What is the stakeholder's level of understanding of your topic? Is the stakeholder new to this topic or an authority?
- What are the stakeholder's information needs? Does your stakeholder need high-level, general information or in-depth details?
- What is the stakeholder attitude or perspective on your topic? Is the stakeholder supportive or opposing?
- What is your objective of presenting the A3 to this stakeholder? What do you want to achieve?

Finally, there are five challenges you need to manage when working with the A3 tool:

1. When several people are working on the project, one person should be the project owner, thus also the owner of the A3. The question is how the other people will get access to the A3 and its updates. In some companies, the issue tracking system is used to distribute and remind people of activities. This could be a solution. Another is that the A3 is placed on the daily management board, so that everyone who needs to can go there and read. If so, don't forget that the owner needs to indicate when they have made a change in the A3.
2. It is easy to lose an A3. We learned this from a company where we became a little fed up the third time we got there and management didn't bring the A3 to the meeting. Someone had left it back home on the kitchen counter. However, if you work regularly with projects and apply Nemawashi in practice (see Section 5.6), the risk of this problem arising is quite small.
3. Sometimes, it is more fun developing and refining the A3 itself than working on the actual project. One solution could be to schedule sessions where you focus on learning with regard to process improvements. You may then refer all proposals related to refining the A3 to that particular session and concentrate on the project during the other meetings.
4. Another problem with the A3 tool is breaking things into objectives. After all, an A3 is not independent; instead, every A3 is part of a hierarchy beginning with the organization's visionary target condition. The result is that experiments/activities to be carried out at one level in the organization turn into an objective (hence a new A3) at the next level. The fact that the A3 is frequently included in a larger context means that changes may have consequences. One way of managing this is to combine the A3 methodology with X-matrices (see next section).
5. Finally, the format may be perceived as limiting. One way of creating more space is to create attachments to the A3. At one extreme, the A3 may have a detailed report as an attachment (e.g., a comprehensive analysis of the current condition). This is not a problem in itself, as long as the reader of the A3 gets the whole picture simply by reading the A3. In such a case, the attachments simply offer more depth. If it is impossible to understand the A3 without reading the attachments, the

very notion of an A3 has been botched. A company that the research team has worked with went from a 100-page strategic plan to an A3 with attachments running the same number of pages. This difference may seem small but was in reality significant. In the later version, the authors had to summarize the strategy on the A3. This enabled them to identify a number of logical inconsistencies in the plan. Hence, the A3-driven version eventually ended up containing materials other than those in the first strategic plan. In addition to improving the quality of the strategy, the A3 also served as an effective summary, thus making it much easier to get the message across.

Hence, it is no easy task summarizing how to analyze and solve a challenge on an A3 sheet of paper. In the world of lean and Hoshin Kanri, there are many stories about what an A3 may look like and how it may be used. A common theme in these stories is that it takes time to learn how to best use the limited space on an A3 sheet of paper. The fact that you have to experiment and change means that it is not a bad idea to use a pencil when working with an A3. This makes it a living document.

In what is perhaps the best-known book on A3s, John Shook's *Managing to Learn: Using the A3 Management Process to Solve Problems, Gain Agreement, Mentor and Lead* (2008), the author presents the following advice:

- Don't worry about using a pencil, pen, or your computer. What matters is that you use some form of system.
- Don't get stuck on formal details. What matters is the content, not the format.
- Ensure that you get your message across. Spend time making the A3 as easy to read as possible.
- Make it messy. The more people writing in your A3, the better. The more interest your A3 arouses, the more impact it will have.
- Use the A3 to control meetings. Gather the participants around the A3, thereby creating focus in the meeting.
- Use the A3 to confirm agreements. Write down agreements made on the A3, thus turning it into your shared protocol.
- Store experiences for reference and to exchange experiences by means of the A3. The A3 is a physical object that can be mounted on a wall and it describes a whole picture, a story. Our computers are more like black holes where we dump document after document, after which we avoid looking at the hole for fear of drowning in it.

7.5.2 X-Matrix

An X-matrix is another way of visualizing the strategy for the entire organization on a single piece of paper. In several organizations that we have encountered and that work with Hoshin Kanri, X-matrices have been used as a way for the management team to create an overview of the management process. In such cases, the X-matrix often serves as an agenda for the management team meetings. Just like an A3, an X-matrix is based on the PDCA logic. In addition to the overview offered by an X-matrix, another advantage is that it highlights a clear focus on measurable objectives.

An X-matrix consists of four headings, where *what* drives *how far*, which, in turn, drives *how*, in turn driving *how much* (see Figure 7.8).

In fact, you can start anywhere in the matrix, but the most natural approach is to start by entering *what*, meaning what is to be achieved in the next three to five years. In this year's process, the next step will be to determine *how far*; in other words, what must be achieved this year in order to eventually achieve the vision (this corresponds to the P in the PDCA model). Once *how far* has been determined, it drives the *how* question above the X (i.e., which overall activities should be carried out in order to achieve this year's objectives). We here write "overall activities," as we assume that this is the X-matrix used by management. The right-hand side of the matrix presents the critical values set for following up activities

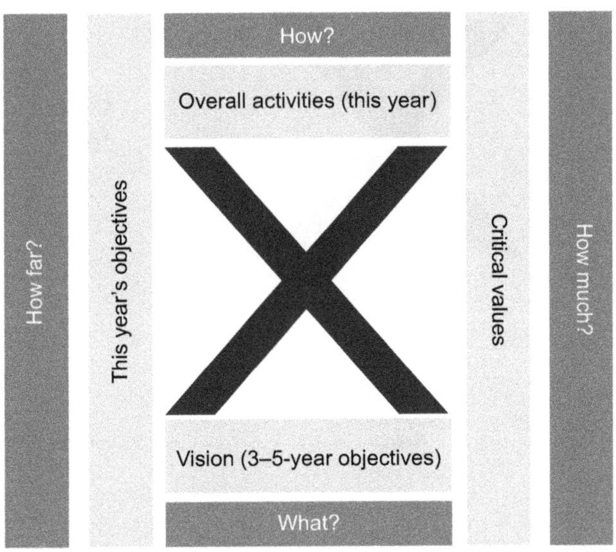

Figure 7.8 The Core of the X-Matrix

during the year (*how much*, which corresponds to the D in PDCA). The critical values thus also describe the KPIs used. Finally is the feedback to *what*, the somewhat longer-term objective (corresponds to the A in PDCA).

The X-matrix doesn't end here. Figure 7.9 shows a more complete X-matrix. We have now added rows in which you can fill out the activities linked to this year's objectives, critical values (KPIs) to be achieved and the long-term results to be achieved.

In addition, there are also four boxes denoted *relationships* (A–D). In these boxes, you should indicate how the different parts of the matrix are connected. The idea is that the vision-oriented result below the X (result 3–5 years) should be linked to this year's objectives through the box called relationships C. In cases where there are links between a long-term objective and one of this year's objectives, this is marked by a cross in the relationship matrix (some people/organizations use numbers). Likewise, relationships between all four parts may then be indicated in relationship matrix A–D.

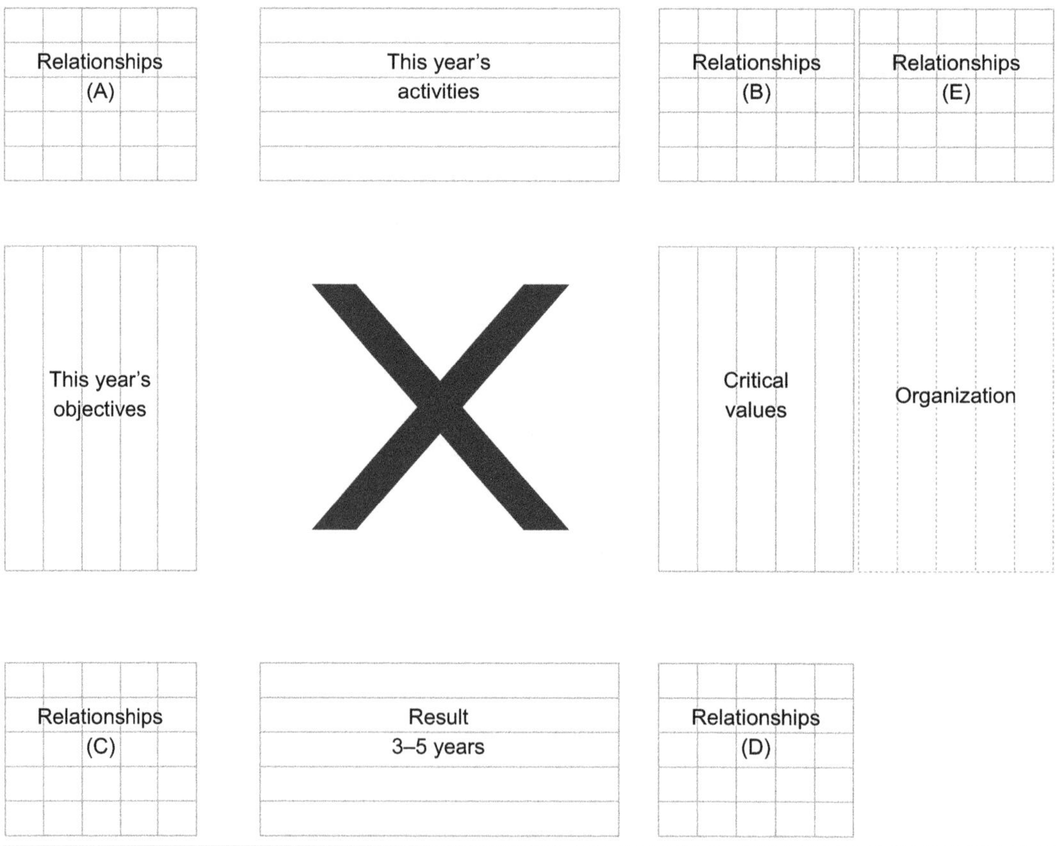

Figure 7.9 The X-Matrix

There are two additional boxes. The people responsible for the one-year activities are to be named under the heading *organization*. Under *relationship E*, it should be indicated with a cross how these individuals are linked to the one-year activities.

Södra Älvsborgs sjukhus (SÄS) has used the X-matrix logic since 2012. Their X-matrix for 2017 is shown in Figure 7.10.

At SÄS, the strategic focus areas play a key role. Some of the five areas include "injuries during care should be minimized," "timely care" and "increased patient involvement." These focus areas control the overall strategic activities to be carried out. In 2017, these included "establish daily follow-up and control in the urgent flow" and "deepen interaction with patients." These activities were then related to that year's critical objectives, such as "care within 90 days." Finally, as shown on the right-hand side of the figure, SÄS had related its objectives to the units/functions concerned. Some were highly affected by a specific objective, thus receiving a three in the relationship matrix, while others were not affected at all, thus receiving a zero.

As you can see, the way in which SÄS applies the X-matrix doesn't look exactly like the model we presented earlier. This is not uncommon but rather a positive sign, as SÄS has taken a model and adapted it to their own unique organization. At SÄS, the X-matrix serves as management's strategic map, which they regularly return to during the fiscal year.

However, the X-matrix is not just a tool for the management team. Just like with A3s, it is possible to create a hierarchy where activities are gradually broken down into the organization. We have tried to illustrate this in Figure 7.11.

Figure 7.10 The X-Matrix of Södra Älvsborgs sjukhus (SÄS)

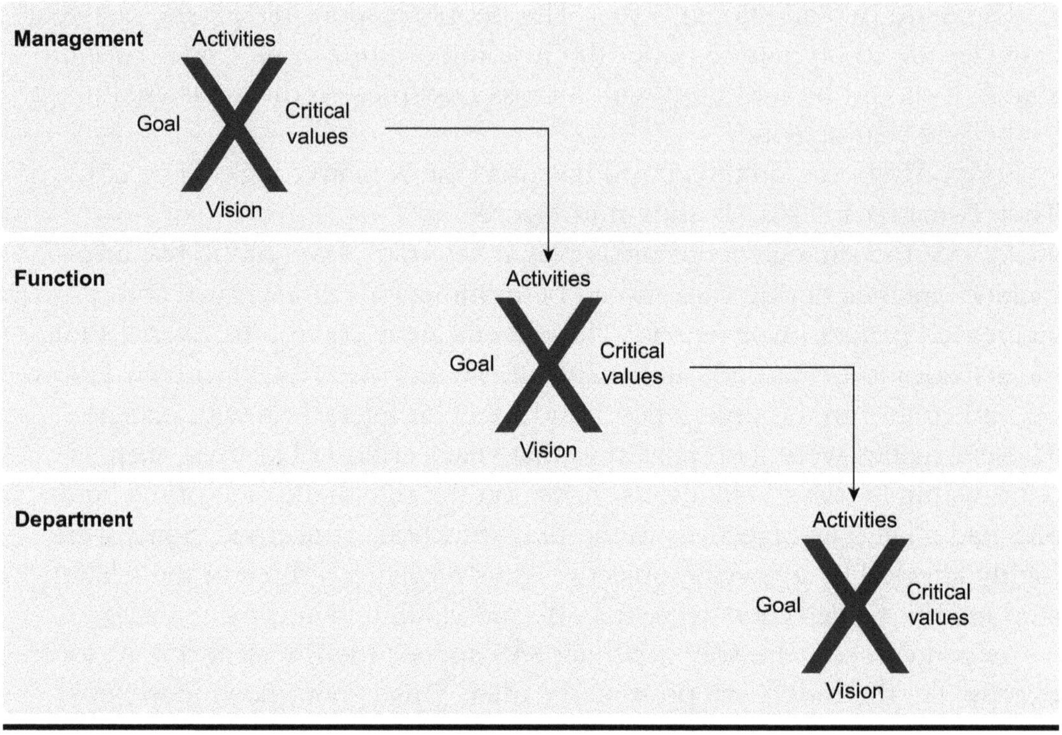

Figure 7.11 Breaking Down an X-Matrix in an Organization

There are different opinions with regard to X-matrices. The advantage is that an X-matrix creates an overview of the strategy work. You could say that you summarize many different A3s. This overview also clarifies the contractual aspect. The X-matrix turns into the contract ending the Hoshin phase of Hoshin Kanri.

Those who are more critical of X-matrices claim that its use as a reporting format means that the PDCA approach is lost and that measurable aspects end up in focus at the expense of softer values. Critics also fear that the X-matrix contributes to too much focus on the Hoshin part in the Hoshin Kanri process. In other words, the negotiations on what should be related to what in the matrix become more important than actually agreeing upon and carrying out activities.

7.5.3 Sunburst Diagrams

In the case of the Lindbäcks Group (see Appendix 1), we describe their strategic process. They use an alternative to the X-matrix, a so-called sunburst diagram. This represents an easy way for management to create an overview of the strategy work. Figure 7.12 shows what a sunburst diagram

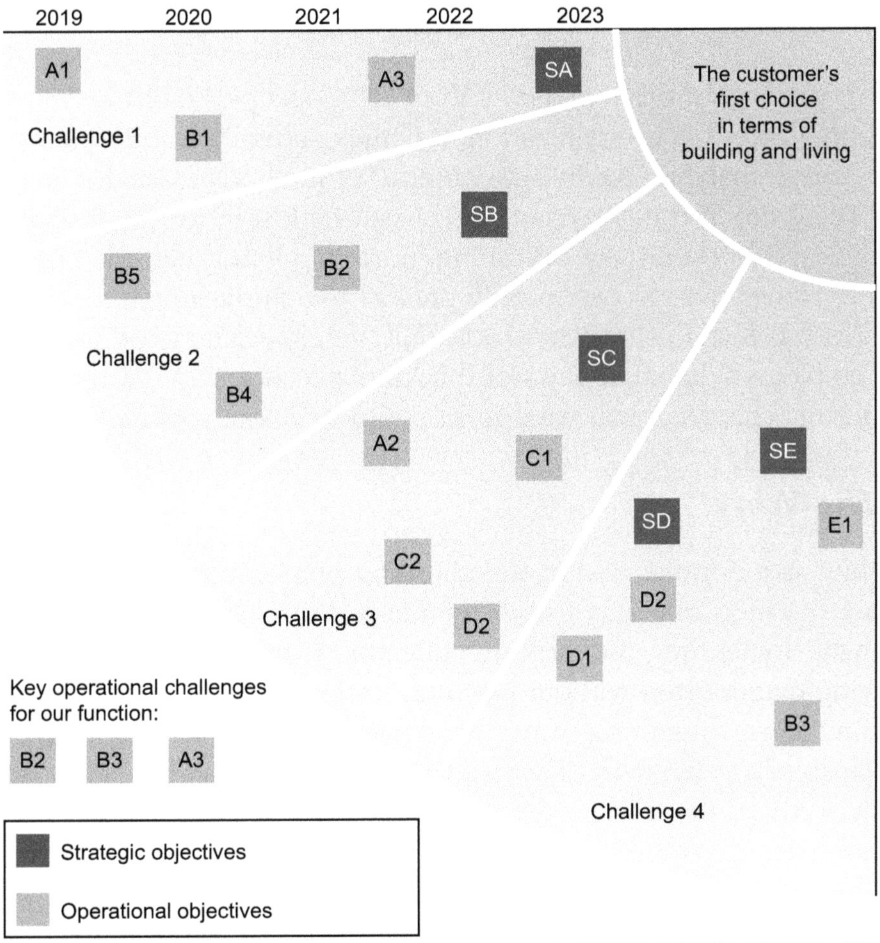

Figure 7.12 The Lindbäcks Sunburst Diagram

may look like. The vision of the Lindbäcks Group constitutes the "sun." The "sunbeams" define the four major challenges that need to be overcome in order to achieve this vision. One or more strategic objectives have been identified in each area (in this case SA–SE), and these strategic objectives have been linked to one or more operational objectives. For example, A1 is an operational objective linked to the strategic objective SA.

The sunburst diagram represents a living document at Lindbäcks, as it is followed up throughout the year and is continuously communicated within the organization. The right-hand side of the figure also shows the most important operational objectives that one of the functions in Lindbäcks is working on during the year. Hence, the sunburst diagram is not only alive at the level of the management team; it also guides the functions in their daily work with strategy.

7.6 Systematic Root Cause Analysis

As shown previously, the P-phase of the PDCA occupies half the A3. When working in a fact-driven organization, it comes naturally to prioritize systematic root cause analyses. An infinite number of methods exists for analyzing causes. There are also many examples of getting lost in the "tool swamp" and the analytical tool eventually becoming more important than the challenge to be solved. Hence, we choose to only present two fairly simple tools illustrating the Hoshin Kanri principles—tools that are especially good for questioning the employees' habitual ways of thinking. See Box 7.13, "Want to Learn More?" in this chapter if you want to know more about root cause analyses.

7.6.1 Five Whys

"Five whys" is a popular tool in the planning phase. It is based on the most important question one may ask: Why? Many young children are good at asking why. Sometimes, they ask this question over and over again, like a self-playing piano, often without listening to the answer. But they usually absorb and learn something from the answer. As we grow up, we for some reason learn not to ask why. This is probably because we are supposed to know most things or because we risk being perceived as difficult. Perhaps your classmates don't enjoy the break being cut shorter as you ask the teacher too many why-questions?

That is why "five whys" is good, since it teaches us to once again stop and think. Not going off and finding whatever solution seems to work but instead being a little more thoughtful and identifying what is truly important.

Let's take a simple example concerning the challenge of getting Philip to be on time for work. One can easily imagine the situation: the supervisor wonders why not everyone is present.

1. *Why wasn't everyone present at 7.00 a.m.?* Philip was late.
2. *Why was Philip late?* The wake-up app on his smartphone didn't wake him up.
3. *Why didn't the app work as intended?* The phone wasn't charged.
4. *Why wasn't the phone charged?* Philip forgot to charge the phone before he went to bed.
5. *Why did he forget to charge his phone?* He was too tired.

The effect of this short "why-exercise" is that we can reformulate the initial challenge concerning being late for work into a new challenge: How is Philip to make sure that he is not so tired that he forgets to charge his phone? Based on this new challenge, you may then jointly consider what the solution might look like. Perhaps the phone should have a feature (an additional app?) warning Philip when the battery is running low. Perhaps this feature can be linked to Philip's wake-up app, so that if there is a warning if a wake-up call is scheduled in the next 12 hours. Or perhaps Philip needs a raise so that he is able to buy a new phone with a better battery. Alternatively, the charging feature may be improved (wireless charging?).

We wrote above that "five whys" is good as it makes us stop and start analyzing. But the point of this tool is deeper than that. The point is to identify a *root cause* of the problem. If you address the root cause, the problem will be solved and, most importantly, it will not reoccur.

A few things are important to keep in mind when performing "five whys" analyses. If, on the other hand, the answer to the second why-question in the earlier example had been that Philip hadn't received the message that his working hours had been altered, then the analysis would have taken a completely different path. The answer to the first why-question is thus crucial for the entire analysis. This means that it is important to test different answers and see where they take you in the subsequent answers. It has somewhat jokingly been suggested that the why-analysis should be supplemented with a "because-analysis" in order to emphasize that the answers to the why-questions should also be analyzed to assess which path offers the most complete solution to the challenge. So, when performing this test of different answers to the first why-question, it is a good idea if you cover different answer categories to determine which one is the most reasonable.

If you want to expand and strengthen the "five whys" model, you will find several ways of doing so. One is to clarify the framework for the first-level answer to the why-question by applying MECE segmentation (mutually exclusive and collectively exhaustive). The objective of this segmentation is to identify a sufficient number of answers to the first why-question to exhaust all relevant possibilities, while at the same time avoiding overlapping answers.

An additional way of creating structure in the analysis is to apply a structured battery of questions. Some variants we have identified include

- 4W—what, where, who, when
- QCD—quality, cost, delivery
- 4M—man, machine, material, method
- 4P—product, price, place, process

7.6.2 Fishbone Diagram

Fishbone diagrams (or Ishikawa diagrams[6]) offer another opportunity to analyze the challenge. A simple way of using fishbone diagrams is to use post-it notes. The point of departure is the initial challenge. If we assume that the analysis is done in a group, you may, depending on the number of participants and the amount of time available, distribute a number of post-it notes to the participants. They then take some time and think about the question: *Why is the initial challenge important?* If you want the discussion to be somewhat structured, you may base it on a few response categories. For example, a common approach is to use 8M (man, machine, material, method, measurement, mission, management, maintenance) as a point of departure.

It is important that the participants take some time before they start writing down their answers on the post-it notes to ensure that the answers are thoughtful. When finished, the answers are placed on a fishbone diagram as shown in Figure 7.13. A "bone" can represent one of the 8Ms described earlier.

The fishbone now created serves as a good starting point for further discussions on the root cause of the challenge. Unlike "five whys" analyses, multiple answers to the why-question may be discussed simultaneously and it is possible to link the answers to each other. After discussing this with the group, it is also possible to prioritize the causes. From here, it is only a short step toward designing experiments. These experiments can lead to increased knowledge of the challenge and thus be part of the gathering of knowledge taking place during the planning phase. When you are finished with the entire root cause analysis, you may obviously design experiments/activities addressing the actual challenge. We have summarized this process in Figure 7.14.

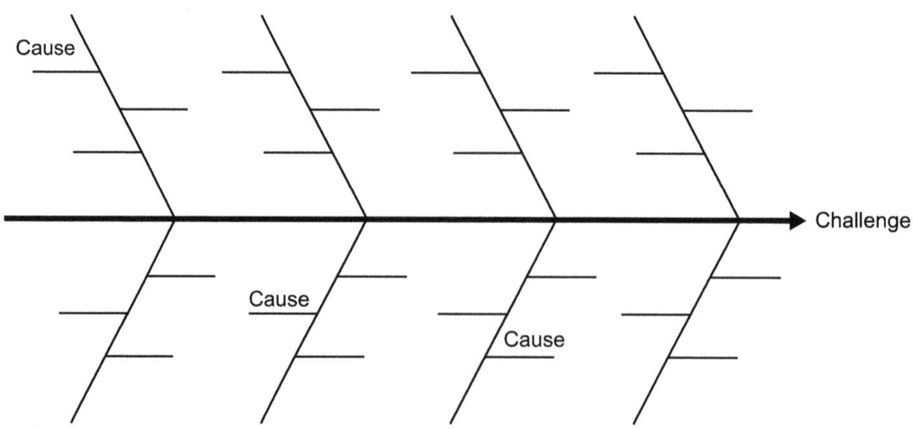

Figure 7.13 Fishbone Diagram

Why	Identify the causes of the challenge
How	**Step 1.** Write down your challenge on a piece of paper (flip chart or similar). Ask the question: What are the possible causes of the challenge? Write on post-it notes. Perhaps use 8M (man, machine, material, method, measurement, mission, management, maintenance) as inspiration when it comes to identifying causes. **Step 2.** Sort the causes and put them in the diagram. Indicate relationships between causes by grouping these on the bones.
Example	We modify the example of Philip on the basis of the 8M structure.

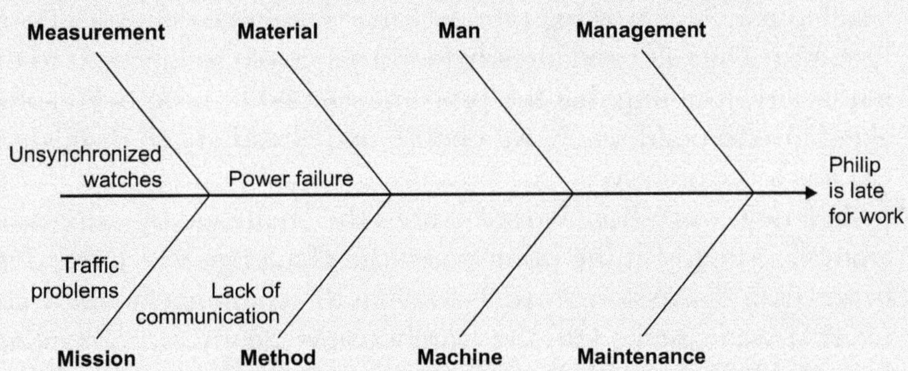

Figure 7.14 The Fishbone Diagram—The Process

A fishbone analysis is easier if the challenge is clear, exhaustive and prioritized by all participants. If this is not the case, the analysis may result in the challenge being rewritten or altered. It thus makes sense to begin the analysis by carefully discussing the challenge. In Box 7.10, we present an example of how a well-conducted fishbone analysis resulted in the original challenge being developed and refined.

There are times when it might be better to start with a *reverse fishbone diagram*. The methodology is the same as described earlier. Instead of searching for the root cause of the challenge in focus, you evaluate the challenge itself. The question asked concerns which objectives are at risk if the challenge is not solved. Depending on the objectives at risk, it is more or less important to prioritize the challenge. The analysis may lead to

- The challenge is given a lower priority and another challenge is analyzed
- The challenge is reformulated to become more important and causes are analyzed
- The challenge is given a high priority and an analysis of causes is initiated

BOX 7.10 THE LEAKY ROOF CAUSING THE WAREHOUSE TO SHRINK

AKC was a small family-owned business in which the management team was identical to the family of owners. In relation to one of the first meetings in the project, AKC faced an urgent challenge: the roof in the warehouse had started leaking. When we started analyzing the challenge together, it emerged that management felt that the warehouse was too small to handle a growing product range and large deliveries from South-East Asia. The CEO had already found a suitable facility next to the existing facility, meaning that the problem seemed to have been solved. The alternative to build a new warehouse had already been dismissed by the CEO as too expensive.

In a new workshop, we structured the challenge by using a fishbone analysis. Already at the point when the challenge was to be described, however, a discussion arose as to what the challenge actually consisted of. That water seeps into the warehouse is clearly a problem, as goods may be damaged. At the same time, the issue of a great amount of capital being tied was raised, in addition to the fact that many mistakes were made in the warehouse and that the work there was irrational. The urgent challenge, the leaking roof, thus triggered a broader analysis.

There was a great deal of engagement in terms of determining facts regarding stock management (e.g., amount of item numbers, volumes, picking frequencies, etc.) for the next meeting. At that meeting, management started formulating a new target condition, which meant an increase in both turnover rate and fill rate. Based on the target condition, a number of activities were agreed upon: (a) moving the warehouse to the new facility; (b) new inventory planning to simply finding and making the picking work more rational with shorter walking distances; (c) finding a labeling system where both the location in the warehouse is indicated as well as a picture of the product, something that simplifies picking the right product; (d) reviewing the purchasing policy. Management also considered whether it would be worthwhile ordering from Europe in smaller shipments but at a slightly higher price.

Three months later, the first three items were fully implemented. The management team had also involved more employees who were very engaged when it came to the approach. The purchasing policy was initiated, while finding adequate alternatives would take time. A few new

European alternatives had been identified. In addition, the company had partnered with industry colleagues to collaborate in terms of purchasing and sharing their "safety inventories."

According to the management team, the warehouse challenge turned into an aha experience. They discovered that the obvious solution to a narrowly formulated challenge could be expanded to address a large number of related challenges, such as capital being tied up, delivery reliability and irrational inventory management. In a systematic fishbone analysis, they got an overview and several birds could be killed with one stone. The foundation for challenge-driven strategy work had been created, and the next step was to formulate a more visionary challenge.

Box 7.11 presents an example of how to start with a challenge and identify its significance. Based on different claims related to the challenge, the different objectives can be grouped into a reverse fishbone diagram, thus helping management decide whether to prioritize the challenge. Here, we imagine that two claims come up in the analysis but are outside the direct discussion. These claims should immediately be "parked" so that they don't take the analysis in the wrong direction.

BOX 7.11 CHALLENGE AND FISHBONES

Challenge: *We have received a customer complaint regarding an incorrectly assembled product.* Is this an important challenge?

Claims related to the challenge:

- This customer is our second-largest customer (30 percent of sales).
- We have a customer satisfaction target at 95 percent.
- We have a quality target of at least 99.5 percent error-free deliveries.
- We have a 10 percent cost savings target, including fewer scraps.
- Our goal is to manage customer complaints within two weeks.

Claims not directly related to the challenge (which are thus "parked," meaning addressed at a later date):

- Our customer records need to be updated. Contains incorrect contact information.
- The product in question has an outdated design.

7.7 Information, Transparency and Visualization

At the beginning of the book, we linked Hoshin Kanri to the general trend toward "open strategy"—a trend resulting in strategy work becoming more inclusive and transparent. So far, we have primarily focused on the inclusive aspect in the chapters describing how to organize the Hoshin Kanri process. Hence, the time has come to focus on transparency.

Transparency may concern many different phases in the strategy work. One way of being transparent is to talk about the results of the strategy work; for instance, to present the organization's strategy at a staff meeting or to make parts of the organization's strategy documents available to all employees, such as in the Lindbäcks Group's sunburst diagram. Material on the organization's strategy, such as business idea, vision and values documents, can also be posted on the website where other stakeholders may also access it. Transparency can also be applied to the ways in which strategy work is organized (i.e., processual transparency). For example, management may invite employees to participate in one of the first steps in the strategy work. It is not uncommon that the strategy work is designed in the form of a larger project, either to complement the annual strategy process or to start working on a neglected process. In any case, great symbolic value is found in initiating strategy work, and if all (or many) employees are also invited to participate in, for example, the initial brainstorming, this sends an important signal to the organization. For example, in a college we are familiar with, more than a hundred workshops were arranged where all employees were invited to brainstorm regarding key areas in relation to the future strategy.

Our view is that most organizations are satisfied with this kind of transparency. Only relatively few organizations are transparent in terms of what happens after all ideas have been generated and the final strategy is to be formulated. This form of initial and partial transparency is problematic as it raises more questions than it answers. Employees who are informed of the current strategy and invited to the process of coming up with ideas for the upcoming strategy could easily become disappointed when there are no traces of their good ideas in the final strategy. Of course, everyone understands that priorities need to be made, but it is essential to explain how priorities have been made and why.

As shown in previous chapters, the Hoshin Kanri model aims to reduce these problems by all employees owning their activities and understanding how these relate to the overall challenges of the organization. This creates inclusion and transparency in the organization. Even more transparency is achieved through visualization.

We have deemed visualization to be one of the principles in the visionary Hoshin Kanri condition. By visualization, we refer to both transparency (everyone can see) as well as the format (easy to see). Well-executed visualization results in engagement and enables increased learning.

Nevertheless, we should not ignore the fact that there is frequently resistance to transparency (and inclusion). In some organizations, the "experts" don't want to share their knowledge. There are many reasons for this. For example, one might think that the strategy is confidential, meaning that it shouldn't be made accessible to everyone. This might also be a question of power based on the familiar adage that knowledge is power. Visualization is based on the opposite approach: inviting employees to participate in decision-making processes leads to better decisions and even better execution. There may be significant resistance to transparency, which is why it is important to emphasize this dimension in the strategy work. If you choose a specific challenge as the point of departure for your strategy work (see Chapter 4), communicating and being transparent with regard to the challenge, the working process and the results are just as important as succeeding in solving the actual challenge. If working with the challenge alters values and behaviors in the organization, this is frequently more valuable than solving the specific challenge.

Visualization is often equated with whiteboards, which are almost always found in production, since the obvious first step in a manufacturing operation is to organize production by illustrating the workflow on a board. In an organization with a good culture with regard to developing, the board doesn't just become a scoreboard. The important thing is not to point out who is good and less good. The important thing is that the flow works, that organizational bottlenecks are identified and that the potential for development is utilized. Consider what we discussed in Section 2.1.4 on process orientation.

But why are these boards only found in production? In fact, it is probably more important to visualize other, more abstract processes than production. In many of the organizations we have worked with, they put up a whiteboard for the administration, which had significant effects. Suddenly, the administrative work became tangible and everyone could see that, for

BOX 7.12 TRANSPARENCY IS INCLUSIVE

When one of us was given the opportunity to participate in Business Unit Wireline Systems in Ericsson's strategy process in the late 1980s, he was given access to one of the 20 numbered and classified binders containing last year's strategy documents. A few years later, the strategy work had changed fundamentally. Strategy workshops had been conducted involving more than a thousand people. In particular, many more functions were involved than what had previously been the case. Even key customers were included in the work. The final document was an A3, with attachments. The management team used the objectives and challenges as an agenda for their meetings. This catchball process also operated one level below the management team. At the subsequent level, however, the results were mixed.

example, a customer complaint case had been dragging on for quite some time. Figure 7.15 shows a picture of Johan Ahlin, CEO of Dörr & Portbolaget i Vittaryd. He is looking at the company's latest experiment—a board illustrating the company's administrative process, from order to production. Below the board, they have mounted a stand where customer orders move between the different steps. The board shows the dates when the different steps are completed. The board and the stand are located right at the entrance of the administrative offices, enabling everyone to see what the situation looks like, what is going according to plan and what has been delayed. The board and the stand cost a total of SEK 400. Johan sees it as an experiment.

At SÄS, they initially placed their X-matrix and related boards in a staircase to increase transparency. Unfortunately, there were problems in terms of space when the management team was to meet around the boards, resulting in them eventually having to move them to a management room. However, the content is still being communicated throughout the organization but now via the intranet. In other words, visualization and transparency create pressure in the organization to perform. You can't hide things, which is easy when you are sitting in an office behind a closed door all day long.

The whiteboard serves as an information carrier but also as a tool creating discipline and, not least, serving as a meeting point. This meeting point is important as it creates social cohesion and enables those who are not directly affected by various issues to contribute with information.

Figure 7.15 Visualizing an Administrative Process

The A3 is also a way to visualize. By focusing and condensing extensive reasoning on an A3, it is possible to create visibility and transparency. The problem with the A3 is that the physical format makes it difficult to share with a lot of people; that is, unless you copy and distribute it after each update. An obvious solution is to digitalize it. This makes it easier to work with an update, but perhaps a dimension is lost when you can't sit down and work on the A3 in a small group. Might this be a question of different generations?

We have often been asked whether there are any IT tools that may serve as support in Hoshin Kanri efforts. In these cases, our answers have been quite vague. There are obviously many IT tools that may be useful. For example, all modern business systems have a case management system, either integrated or as an additional module. Such a system may be useful in keeping the organization organized and having structure in all its activities. Without having carried out any systematic search, we have also encountered more specific IT-based tools designed to manage strategy work. Some of these have great potential. However, when we speak to users, our suspicions were confirmed. These tools do not solve any problem. It helps those who already have order and structure in their work. If you don't, there are consultants who will willingly help you.

But then it is so easy to fall into the tool trap and think that a tool (or consultant) will solve the problem. This assumption seems to be based on a notion that we may outsource thinking (perhaps AI will enable this faster than we think). So, first plan the process. Then implement the process so everyone concerned understands the basic principles. *Then*, you can start automatizing the process with IT-based tools. For example, Toyota uses Excel as the basis for its Hoshin Kanri process, which suggests that advanced IT tools should not be the top priority when introducing Hoshin Kanri.

Transparency can also be linked to time. It is one thing to be open and transparent about what happened six months ago and another to be transparent about what is important to address today. In many of the organizations we have encountered, the pace of communication is key. The need to share information quickly is in these cases managed through daily management meetings. This may be seen as a pyramid of meetings. The bottom of the pyramid involves the daily management meetings and the next level is department/function meetings. It ends at the top in a management team meeting. In this way, important information quickly moves up the organizational hierarchy and bottom-up transparency is facilitated.

BOX 7.13 WANT TO LEARN MORE?

Karl Weick is a renowned organizational psychologist who has written many interesting books and articles. The work that affected us the most is his book on sensemaking, which concerns how we understand our environment—a question that may be useful to reflect upon every now and then.

- Weick, K. E. (1995), *Sensemaking in Organizations* (Vol. 3). Thousand Oaks: Sage.

When it comes to A3s, John Shook is somewhat of a guru. His book *Managing to Learn: Using the A3 Management Process to Solve Problems, Gain Agreement, Mentor and Lead* (2008) is popular. Shook addresses the difference between the A3 as a tool for communication and problem solving and the A3 as a management process. He writes, "The widespread adoption of the A3 process standardizes a methodology for innovating, planning, problem-solving, and building foundational structures for sharing a broader and deeper form of thinking. This produces organizational learning that is deeply rooted in the work itself—operational learning" (Shook 2008 p. 1).

The book by Sobek and Smalley (2008) is also an excellent introduction linking the A3 approach to Toyota's management system.

- Shook, J. (2008), *Managing to Learn: Using the A3 Management Process to Solve Problems, Gain Agreement, Mentor and Lead.* Cambridge: Lean Enterprise Institute.
- Sobek, D. & Smalley, A. (2008), *Understanding A3 Thinking: A Critical Component of Toyota's PDCA Management System.* New York: Productivity Press.

There is much more to say about the X-matrix and how it may be used. Here, however, we can only introduce the tool and instead refer to other sources. For example, a short video on YouTube presents the basics. See www.youtube.com/watch?v=7v9yHL8thIU.

If you then want to read more about X-matrices, we recommend:

- Jackson, T. (2006), *Hoshin Kanri for the Lean Enterprise: Developing Competitive Capabilities and Managing Profit.* New York: Productivity Press.

How to address problems and seek effective ways of solving them is a theme that has resulted in a fair number of books. This means that there are numerous interesting works to read. We have come across a book that we find very appealing: Arnaud Chevallier's *Strategic Thinking in Complex Problem Solving.* It explains something that can be made extremely complex in a way that makes the reader feel as if they understand the complexity without learning all of it. Chevallier has adopted a broad approach regarding all steps in the root cause analysis and structured this in accordance with the scientific systematic approach forming the basis of this book. The first step is a thorough analysis of the problem, which includes an initial analysis, a root cause analysis and what he refers to as an analysis of true causes. This is followed by identifying solutions, choosing a solution, selling the solution and, finally, implementing the sold solution. We believe that those of you who don't seek to become an expert on the subject but who want to learn how to efficiently address practical problems will benefit greatly from this book.

- Chevallier, A. (2016), *Strategic Thinking in Complex Problem Solving*. New York: Oxford University Press.

The outcome of problem solving is frequently that a decision needs to be made. Here, an effective problem-solving technique hopefully makes the alternatives clearer, thus making it easier to make and motivate the decision. In practice, however, not all decision-making processes are based on a systematic analysis of root causes. Instead, if you read texts such as Chevallier's book on problem solving, decisions seem to be made in completely irrational ways. Nils Brunsson and Karin Brunsson have written a book analyzing four different logics concerning decision-making, each rational in its own way:

- Brunsson, K. & Brunsson, N. (2017), *Decisions—The Complexities of Individual and Organizational Decision-Making*. Cheltenham: Edward Elgar Publishing.

Visualization is an area arousing interest. There may be different objectives for using visualization. It can be used to analyze a problem, to identify and develop strategic ideas, to communicate a (complex) message, to call into action, to follow up and monitor. Eppler and Platts have written an interesting article in which they discuss these different uses and analyze how to choose the right type of visualization based on your needs:

- Eppler, M. J. & Platts, K. W. (2009), Visual strategizing: The systematic use of visualization in the strategic-planning process. *Long Range Planning*, *42*(1), p. 42–74.

Notes

1. NAICS is the North American classification system and NACE is the system used in the EU. Read more on www.bls.gov/bls/naics.htm (NAICS) and https://ec.europa.eu/eurostat/documents/3859598/5902521/KS-RA-07-015-EN.PDF (NACE).
2. www.ikea.com/us/en/this-is-ikea/about-ikea/vision-and-business-idea-pub9cd02291.
3. https://er.jsc.nasa.gov/seh/ricetalk.htm. Accessed September 3, 2019.
4. The link to research on thought processes is obvious. For example, Nobel laureate Daniel Kahneman (2011) argues for fast and slow thinking. Fast thinking

is described as intuitive and emotional, while slow thinking is said to be deliberate and logical. The PDCA tool systematizes (and streamlines) the slow thinking.

5. 360-analyses are often used in leadership development, referring to interviews with the employee in question but also with managers, colleagues and subordinates. All to obtain the most comprehensive picture of the employee's leadership.
6. After Kaoru Ishikawa, a Japanese quality guru. Other names also used include cause-and-effect and Fishikawa diagrams.

Chapter 8

Some Concluding Remarks

When we started to get interested in Hoshin Kanri, a group of students looked at the subject in an essay. Their approach was to look more closely at Japanese companies established in Sweden. The question was whether these companies applied Hoshin Kanri in their Swedish operations. The result showed that few people in these companies were familiar with the concept, which confirmed our initial reactions when we asked people about Hoshin Kanri. Most people looked like they had no idea what we were talking about.

Through a fellow member in the research project, Mikael Thulin, we came into contact with Ericsson, which had worked with Hoshin Kanri.[1] We also discovered that 3M Sweden factories and obviously Toyota Material Handling in Mjölby used the concept. When we started looking, we discovered Plan Sweden, from whom we learned much about such things as A3s and Kata coaching. We then broadened our horizon and came across the Lean Institute (www.lean.org/), Lean Frontiers (https://leanfrontiers.com/) and Planet Lean (planet-lean.com). Several additional professional organizations likely offer support in terms of improving one's knowledge of lean and Hoshin Kanri. We gradually got in touch with more organizations working with Hoshin Kanri, including Saab Aerostructures, the social services in Jönköping, Södra Älvsborgs sjukhus (SÄS) and the Lindbäcks Group in Piteå. We are very grateful to them for so generously sharing their knowledge and experiences.

We have further reviewed the implementation of Hoshin Kanri internationally by examining academic reports and attending conferences and through our consultancy work. From this, our general impression is that the concept still has great potential, especially in smaller and public organizations.

We have learned a lot about Hoshin Kanri during this journey. Above all, we have learned that what matters is not whether an organization applies

DOI: 10.4324/9781003194811-8

the concept exactly as it is presented in one of the manuals (e.g., this book) or uses the actual term.[2] What matters is striving for the spirit expressed in the seven principles that we have introduced in this book. We would define this spirit as *a way of working with strategy that channels the employees' inherent willingness to contribute to the development of the organization.*[3] If our book leads to more organizations finding ways of increasing the level of engagement in employees when it comes to developing the organization, we have achieved our goal. What if our book would result in Gallup (see Chapter 1) in a few years' time finding in its surveys that an additional 2 percent of permanent employees feel strongly engaged in their work (i.e., going from 15 to 17 percent globally)? This is a vision that would be great to achieve! We will continue to work in this direction. Our hope is that after reading this book, you want to do the same.

We also hope that you have listened to our recommendation and created a folder named "HK strategy work" on your computer after reading Section 3.1 and that you saved your preliminary vision of what you want your strategy work to look like in your organization. If you have not kept on working with this vision, now is the time to reopen the file and see whether what you wrote is still valid. After that, maybe it is time to approach a colleague and start talking about the strategy work (apply Nemawashi). Perhaps there are more people who, like you, want to improve and be a part of developing a new visionary target condition for the strategy work in your organization. Even the longest journey begins with a single step. Why not take that step now?

Good luck in developing your strategy work!

The Authors

Don't hesitate to contact us if you want to discuss the book and its contents! Email: mean@ju.se

Notes

1. Ericsson came into contact with Hoshin Kanri through a strategic alliance with Hewlett Packard (HP) in the 1990s.
2. Kahneman, D. (2011), *Thinking, Fast and Slow.* Macmillan.
3. Dennis, P. (2006), *Getting the Right Things Done: A leader's Guide to Planning and Execution.* Lean Enterprise Institute.

Appendices

Appendix 1

The Lindbäcks Group

Since working with Hoshin Kanri, we have discovered more organizations operating according to these principles, even though they don't always use the term Hoshin Kanri. For example, names such as "strategy breakdown" or "deployment" frequently occur. Or the organization has an entire management system they have named themselves. The Lindbäcks Group refers to its management system as "One Way."

We identified Lindbäcks in 2016 through our contacts in the construction industry and have been following them ever since. We believe that their journey contains a number of interesting lessons, which is why we decided not only to include short illustrations from Lindbäcks in this book but also to write, in collaboration with the company, a comprehensive case. Here is a condensed story about the Hoshin Kanri journey undertaken by the Lindbäcks Group.

The Lindbäcks Group[1] is a fourth-generation family business founded in 1924. All owners work actively in the company. Today, the company is owned by Gösta and Erik from the third generation and their children Stefan, Hans, Anna and Annica. After having worked outside Lindbäcks (and Piteå) for many years, Anna and Annica have recently joined the company as employees and owners, which means that ownership control is under development. Anna and Annica have worked at Lindbäcks since 2019 as heads of digitalization and sustainability.

Today, Stefan Lindbäck is CEO of the Lindbäcks Group, while Hans Lindbäck manages the sales and project development company with five employees. Magnus Edin is CEO of the construction company with about 520 employees and, finally, Markus Holmlund manages the real estate company with 16 employees. In total, the group has 586 employees.[2] These companies are closely linked together, as Lindbäcks Boende designs and develops the properties built by Lindbäcks Bygg. Finally, Lindbäcks Fastigheter manages the properties owned and operated by the group. The idea is that approximately 30 percent of construction activities should be in the form of their own projects. In the fall of 2019, Lindbäcks has two factories: the original factory in Öjebyn outside Piteå and the newly built factory at Haraholmen (in the harbor of Piteå). In addition, the company operates 21 housing projects, mainly in central and northern Sweden. Recently, they have expanded their activities from northern Sweden to the southern parts of the country. The modules are then transported, mainly by trucks, but they also experiment with shipping.

Lean Management Is Introduced

The story of Hoshin Kanri at Lindbäcks began in 2006 as they started to consider lean as a production system. This was a quite natural development as the company in the 1990s decided to focus on building apartments industrially.[3] Top-of-the-line industrial construction means that you need to use the best production methods. Initially, the introduction of lean was tentative and there were a few setbacks. Ola Magnusson, a lean coach who has worked with Lindbäcks since 2008, found that they made the same mistakes as many others. They entered the project somewhat half-heartedly, focusing on tools and methods while ignoring the key element, that lean (and Hoshin Kanri) requires a change in behavior. It is about leadership.

In 2008–2009, they started over. It is no coincidence that this initiative was linked to the Luleå University of Technology (LTU). The collaboration with LTU started already back in 1989, then as a result of management looking for solutions to the crisis facing the company at the time. This is when the idea of industrialized building was born. And as the legislation on building apartments in Sweden was changed in 1994, industrialized building of residential buildings was the way of the future.

LTU was the engine of a major EU project in 2008, which aimed to develop production in the region. It then became clear that Lindbäcks would be one of the participating companies. In 2009, Lindbäcks had decided to fully focus on lean and already worked intensely on introducing 5S,[4] an analytical tool used for creating order and structure at the factory. This was the first step in creating standardized working methods. What was different from the previous attempt to launch lean was that management emphasized the importance of doing this. The CEO at the time, Erik Lindbäck, emphasized the long-term nature of this investment:

> It sometimes takes time to introduce lean. It is a mental transformation, a new way of thinking among employees that may differ from how they have worked during their entire career.
>
> **(Quote from *Byggindustrin*, October 6, 2010)**

Stefan Lindbäck, then factory manager at Lindbäcks Bygg, adopted the role of leader in the company. In his role as project manager for the entire project, where Lindbäcks was one of the participating companies, Ola Magnusson kept a blog during 2009–2010. Here, he reflected upon some interesting observations regarding the introduction of 5S and lean:

> The overall understanding of 5S is better on the floor than in the office, as several groups on the floor started before the office. The result on the floor is more visual since most people start the journey from a lower level. It is harder to convince office staff why things should be labeled, that everything should have a designated spot. I don't know why this is the case. To those of you who dare to label things carefully and think about the smartest place to keep the stuff, I congratulate you! You'll have a better time at work.
>
> **(lean-ola.blogspot.com, October 2, 2009)**

A few months later, he also notes in his blog:

> The engagement of management is absolutely crucial in terms of whether lean is successfully implemented. When the CEO or owners contact [me], the company is already on the right track.

Ola Magnusson says that he was offered a position at Lindbäcks several times before he felt in 2010 that they had made sufficient progress. At that time, Lindbäcks had about 150 employees, which meant hiring a full-time lean coach represented a major investment. When Ola started working, however, he immediately decided to focus even more on lean. Stefan Lindbäck says:

> I marketed lean to the board by saying that we would achieve 30 percent more capacity in three years without requiring additional resources (staff, facilities). The board saw this and they can count, so we were naturally allowed to continue.

However, Stefan admits that it didn't go according to plan; they only reached 15 percent. He continues:

> No, we had bought a consulting service. Six days a month for three years. Bulked up with the best consultants. They forced us to be on our toes during these years. Incredibly good. Purged a behavior. We now had to behave like an organism working in the same direction.

Lindbäcks pioneered industrialized building and was among the first to go all in with lean management. That is why it was not particularly surprising that Lindbäcks in 2010 was the first company to receive the newly established lean award in the construction sector. The accompanying statement emphasized the change in thinking and the active support from management:

> Introducing lean into a company represents a mental transformation that needs to take time. It is based on the active support and determination of management and the full participation of all employees. The winning company has with great determination and clear customer focus involved everyone in developing safer and more predictable processes. The result of this engagement is an organization characterized by lean thinking.
>
> **(The jury's statement regarding the 2010 lean award, which was awarded to Lindbäcks Bygg)**[5]

In response to the question of whether Ola Magnusson would have done something differently when introducing lean in Lindbäcks, he replied:

> Today, I would have worked a lot more with the management team. Taken them hostage and made them drive themselves. It wouldn't

> matter all that much what [area] they work with, the important thing is that they have to explain why they're doing something. Decide what they want to do and why they want to do this.

A few years later, as this case is being written, it is sometimes difficult to remember exactly what happened a few years back. A 2011 article in *Ny Teknik*, which lets an employee speak out, thus presents an interesting insight into the problems that emerged when introducing lean:

> The plumber Fredrik Lund says that he usually makes it work. Today, however, things don't go according to plan and he is somewhat annoyed. "I'm simply forced to deviate from the new methods. I have to do it in my own way," he says. The new standardized working methods typically work when it comes to boards and fiberboards. This time, however, Fredrik Lund has received some unusually skewed and warped beams, which he will assemble to PVC pipes to form a floor module. "I'm sure the standardized methods work well when working with metal parts staying within tight tolerances. Warped and skewed wooden beams, that's another story," he mutters. . . . "We have previously agreed with the consultant. It's possible that we might do so again. But I question his experience with warped boards," says Fredrik Lund. The consultant he is annoyed with is Torbjörn Engberg and comes from the Japanese consulting firm JMAC.[6]

The financial crisis in 2008–2010 was tough for virtually all companies. However, Lindbäcks did quite well. In 2008, their turnover was approximately SEK 500 million and they had 157 employees. The following year, turnover dropped by 20 percent, to then return to the 2008 level by 2010. Things moved quickly after that. The turnover increased by around 150 percent in 2010–2017, while the number of employees increased from about 150 to just over 500.

Hoshin Kanri Is Introduced

In 2014, Lindbäcks started to apply Hoshin Kanri (or the "sunburst diagram" as it is often called internally). The reason Hoshin Kanri was introduced was actually related to the plans for a new factory. The management team visited several companies (Scania, Astra Zeneca, SSAB, Toyota) to get inspiration.

During these visits, they also noted how projects were organized. One of these companies used a so-called sunburst diagram (the details are a bit unclear in hindsight), which offered inspiration. A sunburst diagram appeared to be an excellent way of visualizing your strategy. The diagram consisted of an A2 sheet of paper giving an overall presentation of the company's strategy. (See Section 7.5.3 for a more in-depth description of sunburst diagrams.)

At Lindbäcks, the sunburst diagram is updated annually. Operational objectives are removed once they are achieved. If they have not been achieved, they will be placed in the "backlog," which means that they won't be forgotten but will be achieved during the next year. Likewise, the vision and the strategic objectives are also revised annually. A difference between the operational objectives and the strategic objectives concerns their measurability. An operational objective for 2018 was "new factory according to specification," and the 2017 objective was "zero errors when delivering new homes." Strategic objectives, on the other hand, could be something like "we have the most attractive offering on the market" (2019), an objective that is described in somewhat more detail in the attached text.

The power of visualization is strong. Stefan Lindbäck explains:

> Things get easier for me as the CEO as I'm able to explain how things are related. The board [the sunburst diagram] hangs outside the door here. There, we may explain why it's important to build projects in Gothenburg. Because this is linked to a strategic objective stating that we should have this capacity in three years' time, which means that we have to start sooner or later. It's strong, transparent and understandable. We have hired a large number of people in the last two years. Unless we open up to why you should work with us and what the objective is, they quickly move on. We have to ask them for a dance. That means that we actually have to let the individual join in, poke around and understand. Then you get this feeling of "Yes, this is where I want to work!"

In 2014/2015, however, the use of the sunburst diagram was not fully developed at Lindbäcks. On the contrary, many changes and improvements reportedly have been carried out in the past four years. In order to understand how the sunburst diagram, and thus Hoshin Kanri, was introduced at Lindbäcks, it is important to describe the single greatest strategic challenge they addressed at Lindbäcks during this period: the new factory at Haraholmen.

Haraholmen

Building a new factory at Haraholmen represented a major project. It was a big deal for Lindbäcks—an investment of SEK 550 million for a company with a turnover of SEK 745 million in 2014 would deter most companies. But it was also a big deal in terms of innovation. Previously, the construction company NCC had launched a factory in the middle of Sweden for the industrial production of apartments. However, this factory, launched in 2006, was closed down already in 2008 after severe losses. Now, a relatively small player in northern Sweden was to embark on the same kind of project. No wonder the Swedish construction sector raised its eyebrows.

Ola Magnusson, who was originally employed as the first lean coach at Lindbäcks, was appointed project manager for the Haraholmen project in 2014 (which then began in 2015). Ola had at this point managed the Hoshin Kanri process in the company together with Stefan Lindbäck. He brought this thinking into the new project. Haraholmen thus turned into the great challenge that Lindbäcks could use for practicing the Hoshin Kanri principles. The company's management team became the steering group for the project.

Work began on setting a visionary target condition for the factory based on questions such as: Was a single item flow something to strive for? Should they seek to be the most attractive workplace in Piteå? (The answer was yes to both questions.) These objectives were then broken down. What does being an attractive workplace actually mean? How do others succeed in this? (The result included elements such as a restaurant, a gym and a very welcoming entrance presenting Lindbäcks' history and current condition.) Many interviewees mention a YouTube video shown during a strategy day. It showed how Aston Martin presented a project in a time-lapse format (fast-forwarding a development). The message was that Lindbäcks should show such a video to the world about the Haraholmen project in three years' time. The bar was set high.

However, the investment in Haraholmen was not the only investment. Lindbäcks also invested SEK 50 million in the Öjebyn factory to improve the flow. This means that Öjebyn to some extent became a test facility for Haraholmen. Experiments on new ideas were initially carried out at Öjebyn to then be fully implemented at Haraholmen; for instance, new methods for plastering walls, floors and ceilings, new handling and quality assurance of volumes during coverage and loading as well as an improved logistics solution for outgoing and incoming goods.

Ola Magnusson has now finished the Haraholmen project and is now focusing on management coaching. The factory manager since 2016 is Henrik Hauptman, who suitably has a background at Volvo Trucks. That same year, Lindbäcks also hired Henric Munde, with a background from White Arkitekter, as chief architect at the new factory.[7]

The factory was opened in December 2017 and the first volumes were delivered in January 2018. The launch went well, and after starting with one volume per day, it reached 11–12 per day by the end of the year. During 2019, such an increase has become more difficult, largely due to the market having changed and production thus having become more varied (set-up times are increasing). The current pace is 14 modules per day, while the goal is a cycle time of 27 minutes, which would result in 16 modules per day.[8]

The Haraholmen project was a strategic undertaking that was truly challenging. Many people in the industry started paying attention to Lindbäcks, and for a few years, the company hosted a plethora of study visits. The objective was clear and engaging. As Ola Magnusson puts it now that they have returned more to day-to-day operations, "Maintaining stability is almost more difficult than to develop." It is no wonder that this brought the staff together, not just the management team. At the same time, this project served as an excellent opportunity for putting the principles of Hoshin Kanri to the test: setting a visionary target condition, analyzing the current condition (both internally and in other industries) and prioritizing activities—what was the most important for achieving the objective? That the project had to be followed up and that experimentation and learning occurred on a continuous basis is quite obvious.

Innovation at Lindbäcks

In relation to its size, the company received a great deal of media attention during these years. Not only for the boldness in building the new factory but also for many other innovations. The objective of 50 percent of employees being women, using fossil-free fuels for transportation on roads and using transportation on the water are some examples of innovations in areas where construction companies don't tend to be innovative. If we then add innovations in production and at construction sites, we start to understand the large interest. Linda Rosén (CEO in 2018–2019) describes the culture:

> This is the family where everything is possible. Everything will and should be possible to solve. That is why we have made innovations, both big and small. If there is something in the walls of Lindbäcks, it's ideas. And sometimes, it's not about us making innovations. We just do. The economic situation has also been such that we have been able to experiment. Everything we have wanted to innovate, we have innovated, both big and small.

During 2010–2020, the company was nominated for 12 different awards and won six. A decent outcome!

At an early stage, Lindbäcks decided to allocate 3 percent of its turnover to research and innovation (R&I). In most other companies, corresponding activities are referred to as research and development (R&D). Why the word innovation? Helena Lidelöw is head of construction and responsible for R&I. She emphasizes:

> The term innovation is about taking things to the market. You can engage in research and development and never get anywhere. Innovation is about turning it into a business.

Helena herself represents an interesting example of innovative behavior. With a background at the Luleå University of Technology, she started working part-time at Lindbäcks in 2010. At this point, the company had collaborated with LTU for several years, something that was intensified as a result of Helena joining Lindbäcks. The Lindbäcks website contains a video in which Lars Stehn, a professor at LTU, and Stefan Lindbäck discuss 30 years of innovative collaboration. Today, Helena works full-time at Lindbäcks Bygg as head of construction and is responsible for contacts with researchers.

Structure and standardization are often considered the opposite of innovation and creativity. This is based on the view that the more structured you get, the less innovative you will be. Lars Wallgren, head of logistics at Lindbäcks in 2017–2019, doesn't really see this contradiction:

> If we succeed with Hoshin Kanri, we will also have innovation. Because if we break down our challenges, we create innovative

> solutions. But it's not like those "innovation days" where you sit and come up with new stuff and finish the day with cake and soda. These innovations don't turn into crazy ideas but are more of the kind "what do we need to do?" . . . Obviously, the way we capture the crazy ideas is something we could develop further in our strategy process.

Helena Lidelöw adds:

> I believe that the attitude toward innovation has an impact on the leadership. How open they are to the "wouldn't it be great if . . ." proposals? There are different ways of addressing these. It is possible to be permissive, but it is also possible to put an end to them at a fairly early stage. What you choose to do in small contexts signals what you're like as a leader. I think doing the right thing here is very important if we are to preserve this innovative culture.

Challenges in Hoshin Kanri

As mentioned earlier, many changes have been made to the Hoshin Kanri approach during the four years that the annual cycle has been in use. One theme among these concerns is the level of ambition. How much are you able to do? Or, put somewhat differently, how focused can you be? One example is that during the first years, there were two points of departure for the strategy work. One was based on the Hoshin Kanri model: breaking down the overall vision and identifying strategic challenges. The second way was a little more bottom-up in nature: it was based on value-based deviations in the current operations. Each year, Lindbäcks conducted questionnaires linked to the company values, which served as a way of analyzing the current condition and identifying areas where there was room for improvement. An obvious effect of this questionnaire was that the subsequent discussions contributed to creating more consensus. The reason is that if the group members expressed diametrically opposing views ("I scored it a one while others gave it a five), the obvious question was why this was the case. (Compare the Readiness Analysis in Chapter 3.) This inventory of deviations from the values led to concrete challenges being identified. The process of making things more concrete is exemplified by the company identifying that the value stipulating that what is delivered to the customer should be correct was not always interpreted in the same way. This, in turn, led to a concrete challenge with regard to clarifying in the contract phase what the customer can expect and what the company should deliver. All to ensure that it is easier to deliver the right products.

However, having two sources of challenges became too much to handle, resulting in too many challenges to address. As a result, the bottom-up approach was subsequently toned down, and it was decided to work more strictly with challenges linked to the overall vision. However, the matter was not settled, as Lindbäcks suffers from the same problems faced by many other fast-growing companies. How are the values to be maintained (and strengthened) when there are many employees spread across a large number of workplaces? In the last few years, new material has thus been developed focusing on the company values.

Another way of addressing the issue of focus/level of ambition is the organizational change made in 2018. Instead of producing a sunburst diagram for the entire company, a structure was created in which the parent company created a sunburst diagram in a dialogue with the board. Each of the three operational companies then made their own sunburst diagram based on the three or four strategic challenges they had been given by the parent company. The operational companies thus work with a total of up to nine strategic challenges during the year, but those originating from the parent company are obviously prioritized.

Another side of the level of ambition relates to what happens if not all operational and strategic challenges planned for the year are solved. This may be due to several reasons and must be addressed accordingly. If it is a question of overly high ambitions, the level of ambition needs to be discussed. If external factors have had an impact, the issue concerns how to improve the analysis of the current condition for the next year. If internal factors have had an impact, these need to be analyzed. Sometimes, however, there will be a backlog, where challenges are transferred to the following year. This is not a failure in itself. Without a high level of ambition, you won't be able to reach very far! This is an analysis performed by the management team and the board at the evaluation meeting before beginning the strategy process for the coming year.

In the introduction to this case, we mentioned that corporate governance is being developed at Lindbäcks. This is also reflected in the Hoshin Kanri efforts. According to Stefan Lindbäck, this may be described as up until now, most initiatives in the strategy work have originated from the company's management team and the board has served as a sounding board in this process. The vision has thus not been formulated as an objective by the owners/board to then be broken down by management; rather, management has formulated the target condition. With new owners joining (the sisters Annica and Anna), the aim is for the board to adopt a clearer role in this process in the future.

Another challenge concerns the pace of the work. Lindbäcks has for a long time worked based on daily management, where feedback from the floor continues upwards in the organization to finally end up at the daily management team meeting. Strategy work is also regularly evaluated (using the expression "progress in the challenges"), but the pace is a bit slower. Initially, it was done every two weeks, but they have now started using monthly evaluations. This refers to the evaluations occurring in the management teams of the operational companies. The pace for each function in the different companies varies. Around the beginning of July, a more thorough evaluation is performed, and depending on how the work has progressed, resources can be reallocated to challenges that have not progressed as planned.

As the year is about to end, the CEO of the parent company then calls a management team meeting in which the CEOs of the operational companies meet with the board to discuss this year's work. This meeting, held in late November or early December, also marks the beginning of the strategy work for the next calendar year. The CEOs then take the outcome of the meetings between the board and the management team of the parent company to their respective companies to discuss this with their management teams. At Lindbäcks Bygg, which is the largest company, the same process is then carried out in each function, meaning that the functional manager takes the message from the management team to their function, which, in turn, sets its operational objectives for the year. This process of determining the objectives for the next year takes a few months, and at the beginning of February, the One Way Days are carried out, which serve as a kick-off for the year. In practice, this concerns two parallel processes: an execution process running throughout the year and a planning process running for two or three months.

At the time of writing, Lindbäcks is carrying out an experiment to break the focus on functions in the organization. The aim is to reduce the clear function-based ownership of the objectives. Instead of each function having full ownership of its own operational objectives, all functions are now tasked with taking initiatives to solve the company's operational objectives, which naturally places great demands on negotiating between the different functions in order to avoid duplication of work. Here, we return to the earlier discussion on focusing. If you abandon clear ownership, the level of complexity must go down (i.e., the number of strategic and operational objectives must be reduced). Stefan Lindbäck sets out the vision of the future for Lindbäcks Bygg:

> If you look at the number one in this, Toyota seems to have one strategic objective and perhaps three operational objectives. We have around a total of 15 operational objectives. We are a little too unfocused today, but they have worked with this for a little longer.

Lindbäcks has three lean coaches employed in 2020.

The Future

When you interview management at Lindbäcks, values and leadership are high on the agenda. This makes sense. The company has grown rapidly and is geographically spread out. The two factories, headquarters and 21 construction sites represent a challenge in terms of standardizing. Three core values form the basis of Lindbäcks' values: drive, engagement and knowledge. The fact that these characteristics are emphasized is no coincidence. The concept of "train the trainer" is a recurring theme. It concerns the leaders having the right mindset and living in accordance with the company values or things will not work. Pierre Ek summarizes these thoughts as follows:

> I believe in the notion of teaching people to think. In other words, they are the experts in their profession, but I can help them think more broadly and make them start looking for their own thinking.

In this context, it is clear that the leadership challenges differ significantly. At the beginning of this case, we quoted Ola Magnusson, who commented on the difference between production and the office in terms of introducing lean. At Lindbäcks, they have found that these differences are also significant depending on the employees' background and geographical context. Being a leader in Piteå, with all the resources close at hand, is completely different from being a leader and practicing Lindbäcks' values at a construction site hundreds of kilometers away. Linda Rosén considers how to address this challenge:

> This challenge with so many new employees made the company slow down and take some things from the beginning. Again. Just consider an example. Some of us, more experienced in Hoshin Kanri, have computerized the process, which affects the visualization. We have now decided that we will be strict in terms of using whiteboards. We do this so that everyone understands the processual logic. The idea is to slow down and make sure that everyone is on board before the train once again begins to accelerate.

So, what does this mean for the Hoshin Kanri efforts? Linda Rosén explained in 2019 that the time had come to take the process to the next level. The process was reliable but not sufficiently good. There was a need for a new vision for the Hoshin Kanri process.

In 2019–2020, Lindbäcks faces market-based challenges. The strong economy in the construction industry in 2016–2017 has come to an end and the number of new housing projects has decreased from nearly 17,700 during the second quarter of 2017 to 12,500 in the second quarter of 2020. A drop by 30 percent. This at the same time as COVID-19 posed a new type of challenge. Looking at the entire year, the forecast is that construction will decrease in 2020 as well. This obviously has a major impact on an industrial builder such as Lindbäcks. This challenge is considerable, as the difference between Lindbäcks and traditional builders is that the project-based operations of the latter enable them to scale down their production apparatus during a recession. They simply don't initiate new construction projects and send home their hired workforce. Lindbäcks has a less flexible set of costs with its significant factory investments. Lindbäcks is well aware of these differences and considers them a challenge. Stefan Lindbäck says:

> We have to get rid of all the waste, because we expose ourselves to the pain of riding out the storm by becoming more efficient and efficient. That is the only way for us. Once the business cycle once again improves, we are at a new next level that is slightly better than when we entered the recession.

Appendix 2

Worksheet for Readiness Analysis

Reflect upon and answer the questions presented for each factor. Given the answers, you give your organization (or the unit analyzed) 1–10 points based on your assessment of the organization's readiness with regard to the assessed factor (*low–high*) in terms of introducing Hoshin Kanri.

Factor 1: External Pressure for Change

- Is the organization successful in terms of profitability, achieving budgets and/or objectives?
- Is it possible to work with change efforts in a well-considered and long-term fashion?
- Is the organization's internal and external efficiency satisfactory or are there obvious major problems that need to be addressed?
- If reaching profit, achieving budgets and/or reaching objectives are not at a high level, is this due to the level of external pressure for change?
- If so, does this level of pressure for change guide priorities within the organization and the pace at which you address these?

BOX 8.1 FACTOR 1: EXTERNAL PRESSURE FOR CHANGE

Low = 1	Medium = 5	High = 10	Points
An immediate pressure for change only allowing for short-term change efforts	No clear external pressure for change and/or unclear interpretation of such pressure	Clear pressure for change that allows for long-term development efforts	

Factor 2: Ownership Control

- Is there a clear link between the overall objectives of the organization and how the unit is managed?
- Is the distribution of governance roles clear?
- Are there conflicts of interest among owners?
- Are there clear arenas (steering group, board, etc.) for addressing possible management issues?
- Does there exist a written ownership directive in which the owner's long-term objectives are clearly stated?

BOX 8.2 FACTOR 2: OWNERSHIP CONTROL

Low = 1	Medium = 5	High = 10	Points
Nonexistent or ad hoc governance	Distinct owners, but a lack of clarity in governance intentions No owner directive	Clear, long-term ownership control offering support and adding expertise There exists a written owner directive	

Factor 3: Level of Ambition

- Is the general feeling that you are satisfied with the current state of your organization? Or is there a constant drive to develop and improve?
- If there are no immediate challenges to address, do you create your own "challenges" within the organization?

BOX 8.3 FACTOR 3: LEVEL OF AMBITION

Low = 1	Medium = 5	High = 10	Points
Consensus on being satisfied with the state of affairs	Unclear and at times differing opinions as to whether things are satisfactory	The organization is driven by a clear ambition to develop and improve	

Factor 4: Focus

- Is the focus in your organization short term, long term or a combination of the two?
- Is the organization's focus clear and justified?
- Is the organization's focus well balanced between internal and external challenges?

BOX 8.4 FACTOR 4: FOCUS

Low = 1	Medium = 5	High = 10	Points
No focus	Internal or external focus Clear long-term or short-term development efforts	Balanced internal and external development efforts Well-balanced short- and long-term projects	

Factor 5: Leadership

- Is there a document describing "how a manager/leader should work" in your organization? Is what is written there applied in practice?
- Is there clear leadership in your organization (someone who takes responsibility)?
- Is the leadership style obviously unclear (ad hoc–based leadership)?
- Is the leadership style result-oriented (transactional)?
- Is the leadership style employee-oriented (transformational, prioritizes individual development)?

BOX 8.5 FACTOR 5: LEADERSHIP

Low = 1	Medium = 5	High = 10	Points
Focus on putting out fires Ad hoc–based or absent leadership	Clear transactional leadership	Transformational leadership Encouraging/ coaching and communicating	

Factor 6: Management Work

- Is there a management team in your organization?
- Does it have regular meetings?
- Are there clear roles in the team?
- Are managers in the team representing their function or (together) managing the organization?
- Are these meetings recorded? Are decisions regularly followed up?
- Are there development efforts/learning focusing on the working methods (e.g., by rotating the role of chairperson, etc.)?

BOX 8.6 FACTOR 6: MANAGEMENT WORK

Low = 1	Medium = 5	High = 10	Points
No management team or team has irregular meetings Focus in meetings is on day-to-day operations	Management team exists, but meetings focus on information and operational issues Limited number of discussions on strategy One or a few individuals dominate meetings	Established management team Regular meetings and clear responsibilities Open discussion with a focus on development Members together manage the organization	

Factor 7: Strategy Work

- Is there an established systematic approach with regard to how the organization works with strategy?
- Are several people involved in the strategy work?
- Is the strategy documented? Is it followed up?
- Is there a systematic approach for developing the strategy work?
- Do one or more people decide upon strategic issues?

BOX 8.7 FACTOR 7: STRATEGY WORK

Low = 1	Medium = 5	High = 10	Points
Nonexistent strategy work or in the hands of one or a few individuals No transparency, inclusiveness, or follow-up	No regular strategy work. When appearing the focus is on formulating a strategic plan	Systematic and recurring strategy work Several people involved Continuous follow-up with a focus on learning	

Factor 8: Problem Solving

- Is there a systematic approach with regard to how problems are prioritized?
- Is there a methodology for solving problems?
- Are emerging problems seen in the organization as a threat or as an opportunity for making improvements?
- Is it the manager the "firefighter" or are several (all) employees involved in problem-solving activities?

BOX 8.8 FACTOR 8: PROBLEM SOLVING

Low = 1	Medium = 5	High = 10	Points
Sporadic initiatives No systematic approach Primarily reactive ("putting out fires") The manager solves problems	Problems are often solved where they arise No clear methodology	Well-established methodology Follows a clear problem-solving process (e.g., PDCA) Many people are involved in solving problems	

Factor 9: Body of Knowledge

- Where do you find knowledge to use when solving problems and/or developing your unit? (Your own experience? Your colleagues? Manuals/records? Consultants/externals?)
- Does "we/I know best" apply in your organization?
- Does "call the consultant" apply in your organization?
- Or do you sit down together and get a handle on the problem so that you may then decide whether you yourselves know what to do or whether you need to call in someone from the outside (hence a problem-solving methodology)?

BOX 8.9 FACTOR 9: BODY OF KNOWLEDGE

Low = 1	Medium = 5	High = 10	Points
We ourselves know best	There is a body of knowledge but no systematic generation of knowledge	We find the answers through our problem-solving process There is a clear knowledge structure	

Factor 10: Visualization

- Is information on how the organization is developing offered on a regular basis?
- Have you taken the next step in your organization and visualized the situation by regularly disseminating news, information, measurements and the like on message boards, on monitors or digitally?
- Are there systematically organized daily management boards?
- Is there an established method for how you work with daily management?

BOX 8.10 FACTOR 10: VISUALIZATION

Low = 1	Medium = 5	High = 10	Points
No visualization	Daily management using boards	High degree of visualization: vision, strategic objectives, problem solving, daily management and more Clear link to vision and long-term objectives	

Factor 11: Inclusion

- Does everyone in the organization actively participate in your internal meetings?
- Is the decision-making process transparent and possible to influence?
- Are important decisions explained?
- Do all employees look upon this as something positive?
- Are there systematic improvement efforts to include more people?

BOX 8.11 FACTOR 11: INCLUSION

Low = 1	Medium = 5	High = 10	Points
No inclusion Strategic decisions come as a surprise to many people	The decision-making process is often described by management, but there is limited interest in the organization to participate since the impression is that it is not possible to influence things	Regularly recurring meetings where all/many employees are invited to work with strategic issues Clarity in terms of how the individual contributes to the strategy work	

Factor 12: Individual Follow-Up

- Are there regular routines for performance reviews?
- Are there clear and established ways of measuring performance?
- Is there a (clear) link between the overall objectives/strategy of the organization and the individual goals as determined in the performance review?

BOX 8.12 FACTOR 12: INDIVIDUAL FOLLOW-UP

Low = 1	Medium = 5	High = 10	Points
There is no systematic individual follow-up	There is systematic individual follow-up, but the link to the organization's needs for development is unclear	Systematic individual follow-up with a clear link to the organization's overall objective/strategy	

The Organization's Desire and Capacity

Add up the scores as follows:

BOX 8.13 ADD UP SCORES

The organization's desire: Factors 1–4
The organization's capacity: Factors 5–12

Based on the scores you have received, you then create a rating that gives you a rough indication of the current situation (Figure 8.1).

Desire (1–40)

A Organization with a high level of individual desire to drive development but with great shortcomings in terms of capability **We want to do it, but we don't really know what we can do**	C Organization with a high level of organizational desire and capability to drive development **We can do it and we know what we want**
B Organization without a strong desire and a low level of organizational capability **We can't do it and don't want to**	D Organization with a high capability to drive development but with a limited or fragmented desire to develop **We are capable but don't really know what we want to do**

Capability (1–80)

Figure 8.1 Classifying Your Organization Based on Desire and Capacity

Appendix 3

Worksheet for PDCA Analysis

BOX 8.14 WORKSHEET FOR PDCA ANALYSIS

PDCA Analysis	
Why?	A systematic approach is important for effective problem solving and learning. A common approach also facilitates participation. A standardized methodology increases learning during problem solving.
What?	This method is based on the basic steps of *plan* (background, current condition, target condition, gap, proposed actions), *do* (experiment), *check* (how did it go, what have we learned?) and *act* (what will be the next step?).
Who?	The PDCA tool may be used individually or by a group. It may also be used at all levels in your organization. The thinking forming the basis of this tool is key for Hoshin Kanri, which means that it is beneficial if the entire organization uses the tool.

PDCA Analysis	
How?	
PLAN	Background: Why is solving the problem so important?
	Current condition
	Target condition
	Gap/root causes
	Proposed actions
	Planning experiment
DO	Perform experiment
CHECK	How did it go?
	What have we learned?
ACT	What is the next step?

Notes

1. The Lindbäcks Group consists of several companies. The three largest are Lindbäcks Bygg, Lindbäcks Boende and Lindbäcks Fastigheter. To simplify matters, hereafter we simply refer to the group as Lindbäcks.
2. The information on the number of employees originates from the 2018 annual report.
3. Industrialized building, which includes a substantial degree of prefabrication, is a currently a growing trend in many countries. In the 1990s, this production philosophy was new in Sweden, especially when it came to apartment buildings made out of wood. This video presents what Lindbäcks' production system looks like today, www.youtube.com/channel/UCjN6RQpN6sEaWQVaB0n4mDw. It is produced by DaveCooper.live.
4. 5S is a Japanese method for creating order and structure. In English, each S represents one aspect of 5S: sort, set in order, shine, standardize and sustain.
5. www.leanforumbygg.se/arets-lean-byggare/vinnare-2010-lindbacks.

6. www.nyteknik.se/automation/har-rullar-hoga-hus-pa-bandet-6335793, April 17, 2011. At the time of writing, both Fredrik Lund and Torbjörn Engberg are employed at the Lindbäcks Group. Ola Magnusson and Torbjörn Engberg represent examples of something that happens repeatedly at Lindbäcks: they have used external support and these people have then turned into important elements in the company's expansion.
7. www.pt.se/nyheter/pitea/lindbacks-miljonrustar-fabrik-10280844.aspx.
8. In Lindbäcks' world, 2.35 volumes correspond to one apartment, which means that the goal of 16 volumes corresponds to 6.8 apartments being produced per day at Haraholmen. Obviously, this is subject to the exact nature of the "apartment mix." Lindbäcks' strategic objective is to reach 2,500 apartments per year, which corresponds to 5,875 volumes in the two factories.

Index

Page numbers in *italics* indicate a figure and page numbers in **bold** indicate a table on the corresponding page. Page numbers followed by "n" indicate a note.

For Product Safety Concerns and Information please contact our EU
representative GPSR@taylorandfrancis.com
Taylor & Francis Verlag GmbH, Kaufingerstraße 24, 80331 München, Germany

www.ingramcontent.com/pod-product-compliance
Ingram Content Group UK Ltd.
Pitfield, Milton Keynes, MK11 3LW, UK
UKHW052225190926
475702UK00007B/1209
* 9 7 8 1 0 3 2 0 4 8 2 6 0 *